Visions
of Utopia

TENNESSEE·
THREE STAR BOOKS

Visions
of Utopia

Nashoba, Rugby, Ruskin,

and the "New Communities"

in Tennessee's Past

BY JOHN EGERTON

PUBLISHED IN COOPERATION WITH

The Tennessee Historical Commission

THE UNIVERSITY OF TENNESSEE PRESS

KNOXVILLE

TENNESSEE THREE STAR BOOKS / *Paul H. Bergeron, General Editor*

This series of general-interest books about significant Tennessee topics is sponsored jointly by the Tennessee Historical Commission and the University of Tennessee Press. Inquiries about manuscripts should be addressed to Professor Bergeron, History Department, University of Tennessee, Knoxville.

Second printing, 1983; third printing, 1988.

The paper in this book meets the minimum requirements of the American National Standard for Permanence of Paper for Printed Library Materials. ∞ The binding materials have been chosen for strength and durability.

Library of Congress Cataloging in Publication Data

Egerton, John.
  Visions of utopia.

  (Tennessee three star books)
  Includes index.
    1. Collective settlements — Tennessee — History.
  2. Utopias — History. I. Title. II. Series.
  HX655.T2E37   335′.9′768   77-1509
  ISBN 0-87049-294-2 (cloth : alk. paper)
  ISBN 0-87049-213-6 (pbk. : alk. paper)

ABOUT THE AUTHOR

John Egerton is a native Southerner—a Georgian by birth, a Kentuckian in his childhood and youth, a Floridian during the early 1960s, and a Tennessean since 1965. He is a grandson of one of the English colonists who started the Rugby settlement in 1880. As a journalist and author, he has written articles on a variety of subjects for more than twenty magazines, and has published two books about the South: A MIND TO STAY HERE (1970) and THE AMERICANIZATION OF DIXIE (1974).

For Anne, Skip, and Gra,

beneficiaries with me of a utopian dream

Contents

ILLUSTRATIONS

Photographic credits: Front cover and pages 34, 53 (top), 63, 69 (bottom) by
the author; page 41 (bottom) by James N. Keen; page 29, courtesy of
Indiana Historical Society Library

Visions
of Utopia

1. Four Centuries of New Communities

Athens . . . Rome . . . Carthage . . . Sparta . . . Troy . . . Sardis . . .
Alexandria . . . Memphis . . . Milan . . . Como . . . Paris . . . Bordeaux . . .
Moscow . . . Dresden . . . Dover . . . Belfast . . . Bogota. Cities of the world,
ancient and modern—and also place names on the contemporary map of
Tennessee.

Every state has its "far-away places with strange-sounding names," and
Tennessee is no exception. You can go to Egypt and Persia, to India, to
Denmark, to Cuba and Brazil, and never leave the Volunteer State. The
founders of those towns and villages probably never saw Rome or Moscow or
Bogota or any of the other exotic places whose names they chose, but there are
some Tennessee communities with names that do have a direct connection
with the past. Alamo, the county seat of Crockett County, recalls the heroism
of Tennessee frontiersman David Crockett and the Texas fortress he and
others died defending. Santa Fe, in Maury County, may owe its name to the
same period of nineteenth-century warfare in the West. It is popularly believed that the Tennessee men who went in such great numbers to fight in the
war with Mexico inspired the state's nickname—Volunteer—and veterans
returning from that campaign brought back stories of the battles at Tampico,
Saltillo, and Buena Vista, giving those Spanish names to three new communities in the state. There is also a Montezuma, Tennessee.

Long before the nineteenth century, the land that is now Tennessee be-
longed to its original natives—the Indians—and dozens of cities, towns, and
rivers in the state (indeed, the name Tennessee itself) are reminiscent of those
first Americans. Chattanooga, Tullahoma, Etowah, Sequatchie, Chewalla,
Pocahontas, Culleoka: in bustling metropolises and quiet hamlets alike, the
Indian heritage lives on, at least in name.

Another group of Tennessee towns is distinguished by colorful and descrip-
tive names that stimulate the imagination. Nankipoo, near the Mississippi
River, was inspired by a character in the nineteenth-century Gilbert and
Sullivan comic opera, *The Mikado*. There is a Liberty and a Reverie, a Static

and a Dull, a Harmony and a Prosperity, an Only and a Nameless, a Difficult and a Defeated. There is Hanging Limb, and Peeled Chestnut, and Finger, and Frog Jump, and Tiger Tail. There is Nosey Valley ("Population Varies," says the road sign outside it); and there is Stupidville ("Population 187— Unincorporated As Of Now"), so named by a village storekeeper, allegedly in protest against what he considered the low caliber of local officeholders.

Discovering what's in a name is one way of gaining a better understanding of who we are and how we got here. It is instructive to learn that when the Spanish explorer Hernando DeSoto led the first party of white men into the Tennessee country in about 1540, there was a large Indian village called Chiaha on an island in the Tennessee River a few miles north of the present location of Chattanooga, and the place where DeSoto is believed to have crossed the Mississippi River—identified then as the fourth Chickasaw Bluff—is now the site of Memphis. French and English explorers who came into the territory in the 1600s found the Chickasaws and the Cherokees already here in great numbers, and the Cherokees in particular had a highly organized society. Their seven "mother towns" in the eastern mountains included Tanasi (Tennessee) and Great Tellico (on the site of what is now Tellico Plains), and those towns (also including Toskegee, birthplace of the great inventor of the Cherokee alphabet, Sequoyah) were highly developed and thriving when whites began to arrive in greater numbers in the eighteenth century. A site on the Cumberland River known as the Big Salt Lick or the French Lick was a busy French and Indian trading post almost a hundred years before James Robertson and John Donelson began the Nashborough settlement (now Nashville) on the site during the Revolutionary War.

The first white people to settle permanently in what is now the state of Tennessee were probably William Bean of Virginia in 1769 and James Robertson of North Carolina in 1770. They, and others who joined them in what became known as the Watauga Settlements, later formed an association and adopted the first written constitution among European settlers in America. During and after the Revolutionary War, the Watauga territory was the subject of claims and counterclaims involving its white settlers, the Cherokees, the British, the state governments of Virginia and North Carolina, and the government of the United States. In 1777, the Wataugans asked North Carolina to make them part of that state; the following year, all of Tennessee became Washington County, North Carolina, and Jonesboro, now known as Tennessee's "first town," was established as the county seat.

But the problems of frontier warfare and disputed land claims continued, and the people of the Watauga region became increasingly dissatisfied with their North Carolina connection. In 1784, they held a convention in Jonesboro and voted to form a separate state, to be called Franklin (in honor of Benjamin Franklin). A year later, Franklin's elected legislature met, and under the leadership of John Sevier (later to become the first governor of the state of Tennessee), counties were created, a militia and a court system were set up, a taxing mechanism was established, and Congress was asked to formally recognize the new government. North Carolina's strenuous opposition to the separation was decisive, however, and Congress refused to recognize the new state; by 1788, the government of Franklin had collapsed, and a year later, North Carolina ceded the entire Tennessee territory to the United States. Seven years after that, in 1796, Tennessee became the sixteenth state of the Union.

The leaders of Franklin had wanted to include in it all of what is now known as Southern Appalachia—the mountain counties of eastern Tennessee and Kentucky, southern West Virginia, western Virginia, and northern Georgia. More than fifty years after Franklin failed, another East Tennessean resurrected the idea of mountain unity, and once again came close to forming a new state.

Ezekiel Birdseye, a transplanted Connecticut Yankee who had become a successful businessman in the Tennessee town of Newport, collaborated in 1840 with Jacob Peck, a one-time Tennessee state senator and supreme court justice, in an attempt to form a free labor colony in East Tennessee. Their long-range plan was to join together the mountain counties of five states to create the new state of Frankland, a sovereign entity pledged to industry, free labor, and the abolition of slavery. According to an article by Henry Lee Swint in a 1944 issue of the *Tennessee Historical Quarterly,* Birdseye and Peck sought to merge two reformist sentiments then present in East Tennessee: abolition and secession. The former drew upon small but influential groups of whites who opposed slavery; the latter was a result of pervasive sectional hostility to the political and economic power that had shifted from the mountains to the western two-thirds of the state. The abolitionists and those who felt alienated from the state's power base were not necessarily allies, but Birdseye and Peck adroitly drew upon both groups to form their "free state" movement.

They came surprisingly close to success. A resolution calling for a study of "the expediency and constitutionality" of East Tennessee's secession from the state—and requiring the governor to open discussions on the subject with governors in the adjacent mountain states—was introduced in both houses of the Tennessee General Assembly in 1841. The sponsor of the measure in the Senate was Andrew Johnson, an East Tennessean who later became President of the United States. The Senate passed the resolution by a vote of 17 to 6, but it failed in the House, and the dream of a free Frankland faded and finally died.

Some of the names on the present map of Tennessee can be traced to the arrival of European immigrants in the nineteenth century; other communities established in that same period have since disappeared. One of the latter was a Welsh settlement in Scott County known as Brynyffynon ("the hill with a spring"). A Welshman named Samuel Roberts, seeking relief from hard times in his native country, purchased a large tract of land in East Tennessee and prepared a brochure to advertise it as a new frontier calling to his fellow countrymen. About forty people bought land from him at the equivalent of approximately fifty cents an acre, and in 1856 the first small group of them arrived and began clearing land for a settlement. But only a few families ever came, and only Roberts and his brother stayed. "The courage and tenacity of the Robertses kept alive the dream of a truly Welsh settlement in Tennessee for another decade," wrote Wilbur Shepperson in the *Tennessee Historical Quarterly* in 1959; but when they left, Brynyffynon "was deserted and quickly dissolved into the forests from which the cabins had been hewn." Welsh immigrants came again to Tennessee after the days of Samuel Roberts—as we shall see later. There is also an ancient legend alive in Wales today of Welshmen building smelting furnaces in the Tennessee mountains in the twelfth century.

More successful than Brynyffynon—if no less arduous—was a Swiss colonization venture in Grundy County after the Civil War. E. H. Plumacher, a Swiss government official, was sent to the United States in 1867 to seek settlement sites as a partial answer to overpopulation and economic depression in his native country. President Andrew Johnson, himself an East Tennessean, referred Plumacher to friends of his in the mountains; and a private company from Switzerland headed by Peter Staub subsequently bought up a twenty-square-mile tract of land in Grundy County and promoted it for sale at about fifty cents an acre to Swiss citizens eager to leave their homeland.

The first party of settlers arrived in 1869, and in time more than seventy-five families emigrated to the colony, which was named Gruetli ("a clearing, a meadow"), after a place by that name in Switzerland. The colonists suffered great hardships in the beginning, and the primitive conditions they found there contrasted so sharply with the picture of paradise Peter Staub had painted for them that the angry settlers felt misled and abandoned. But they were determined to succeed, and they built a community that at its peak numbered close to 300 Swiss, a tight-knit and homogeneous group with a strong sense of cultural identity. For nearly thirty years they managed to preserve their German language, their school and church (Protestant), their music and dance, their woodcarving and winemaking skills, and their agricultural way of life. But many of those qualities succumbed to the influences of assimilation and mobility and the changing times, and Gruetli today bears little resemblance to the authentic Swiss village it once was. The original settlers never lost their contempt for Peter Staub, however. One of them told Frances Helen Jackson, a Vanderbilt University graduate student doing research at Gruetli for a master's thesis in 1933, that Staub was, in the opinion of the colony's survivors, "a first-class swindler."

European promoters of land sales in Tennessee and other American states in the middle of the nineteenth century apparently included more than one "first-class swindler." In a brochure called "East Tennessee U. S. A.," published in London in 1842, depressed and oppressed Europeans were invited to buy "fertile meadows, bold limpid streams, evergreen pastures . . . every requisite for comfort, convenience, and pleasure"—in the rugged and formidable mountains of Tennessee.

German-Swiss emigration to the United States between 1840 and 1860 was substantial, and although the foreign-born proportion of Tennessee's population was only 1 percent as late as 1880 (compared to 15 percent nationwide), several communities in the state originated in the nineteenth century as German or Swiss settlements. More than half a dozen of them still exist, among them Gruetli, Germantown, Mosheim, Hohenwald, Belvidere, Allardt, and Wartburg. Wartburg was a substantial land development enterprise that began in 1844 and in ten years attracted close to 1,000 immigrants. Now Morgan County's seat of government, Wartburg has a population of approximately that same figure, but few traces of its German heritage remain.

An altogether different kind of new community in Tennessee in the nineteenth century was the health spa. Middle Tennessee abounds with mineral springs, and more than thirty of them were developed into health and recreation resorts attracting affluent Tennesseans to spend their summers there. One of the first, and by some accounts the finest, was Beersheba Springs in Grundy County. Incorporated in 1839, its first hotel opened that year, and the resort had its heyday in about 1859, before declining during the Civil War. Perhaps the best-known spa was Red Boiling Springs in Macon County. It had several boarding houses and hotels in the 1880s, and both before and after World War I it was a thriving and prosperous summer community. Before a series of disastrous fires, the Great Depression, and the advent of the automobile signaled the end of its good times, Red Boiling Springs had nine hotels, a rich variety of cuisine and entertainment, and its famous mineral waters, reputed to be a cure for almost any ailment from diarrhea to gonorrhea. Among the other watering spas that are still on the map are Hermitage Springs, Eldorado Springs, Castalian Springs, and Bon Aqua; the latter, in Hickman County, was a health resort as early as the 1820s, a decade or more before Beersheba Springs began to attract visitors. Charles B. Thorne, writing about the watering spas in the *Tennessee Historical Quarterly* in 1970, noted that one or two of them still have limited facilities in operation during the summer months, but for the most part, the small, quiet villages have been bypassed by a new generation of vacationers bound for Gatlinburg and Opryland and the bright lights of modern diversions elsewhere.

The contemporary version of the resort community can be seen in the proliferation of heavily promoted land development projects, particularly in the eastern half of the state, that cater to the recreation, retirement, and second-home dreams of the American middle and upper classes. The largest of them has more than 15,000 homesites, and the promotional literature extolling their assets is reminiscent of the "fertile meadows–limpid streams–evergreen pastures" language in that 1842 brochure from London. On the Cumberland Plateau alone, more than a dozen major speculative land developments have sprung up on the mountainsides and in the forestlands of a people who have never known great economic prosperity, and the contrast between the indigenous residents and the affluent newcomers is stark and pervasive. A number of apparent or potential problems related to these developments—problems of environmental impact, water supply, sewage treatment, solid waste disposal, police and fire protection, medical services, and property valuation—are cited in a 1974 report issued by the Upper Cumberland Development District, a regional planning and development agency. The report also describes an adverse social consequence of the new communities:

> The large developments themselves are highly self-sufficient in terms of the particular needs of the residents of the development. One of their selling points is that an almost total play and relaxation environment is provided within the confines of the development (there are some exceptions, notably potable water and health care). . . . Seemingly, the developments are assuming the character of super "country clubs" or resorts for metropolitan residents [and] retirees. . . . The new community residents [come] to relax and play while the established residents carry on working and day-to-day living. The differences in life-style contrasted in affluence and marginal subsistence . . . portray the likely divergence of the communities. . . . There will probably be a high degree of social isolation unless there is ample opportunity to break the barriers.

The Tennessee General Assembly, in an attempt to reduce the problems caused by the creation of these new communities, enacted in 1974 the New

Community Development Act; the law provides for a Tennessee Community Development Board to regulate and oversee the establishment of new communities in the state. As the phenomenon of land speculation and promotion continues, the quality, stability, and permanence of Tennessee's new communities of the present period cannot yet be adequately assessed. Whether they will be the Nashvilles and Knoxvilles of the future—or the Brynyffynons, the Bon Aquas, and the Beershebas—will remain for a later generation of Tennesseans to say.

Not many new communities have come and gone in Tennessee since the beginning of the present century, but there have been a few. For example, there was a Bohemian (Czechoslovakian) settlement on the Cumberland Plateau near Mayland in 1913. Its residents, most of them immigrants who had been struggling to survive in the cities of the North, attempted to farm collectively and to recapture the agricultural way of life they had known in their homeland. Internal dissension quickly shattered their agrarian dream, however, and most of them returned to the cities.

During the administration of Franklin D. Roosevelt, a rural resettlement program brought poverty-stricken coal miners and others into the Cumberland Homesteads near Crossville. The community did not become an incorporated town with an official name, but it was successful nonetheless; several of the original families still live there. Two other unincorporated but distinct communities that have existed in Tennessee for more than twenty-five years are the Amish and Mennonite settlements in Lawrence and Overton counties.

There are older cities, such as Kingsport and Oak Ridge, which have been made over, so to speak, by industrialization and by the massive intervention of the federal government. Kingsport, which was an unnamed settlement when the Declaration of Independence was written, began its "reconstruction" during World War I, and blossomed, ironically, during the Great Depression, when the Eastman Kodak Company initiated expansion of its industrial complex there. Kingsport grew from 12,000 people in 1930 to more than 50,000 by the end of World War II. The renaissance of Oak Ridge resulted from creation of the Tennessee Valley Authority and the Atomic Energy Commission.

Only a handful of place names on the contemporary map of Tennessee have been added in this century. One of those is Norris, a town that was built by the Tennessee Valley Authority in 1933 for construction workers at Norris Dam, the hydroelectric facility named for Senator George Norris of Nebraska, who introduced the legislation creating TVA. Norris, now a town of about 2,000 people, was owned by TVA until 1948, when it was sold at public auction for $2.1 million to a group of Philadelphia businessmen who in turn sold individual properties to occupants as their leases expired. (More recently, TVA has talked of developing a new city, a planned community to be named Timberlake—for Henry Timberlake, a British emissary among the Cherokees in the eighteenth century—but so far, the idea has not materialized because of litigation.) Another twentieth-century name on the Tennessee map is Pressman's Home (identified on some maps as Camelot) in Hawkins County. Developed as the headquarters of the International Printing Pressmen's and Assistants' Union of North America, it once boasted a large hospital, printing facilities, a training school, and housing for several hundred residents; now, it is all but deserted. The name Camelot was given to the community by real estate developers who bought the property from the union.

There is in all of these ventures, spanning more than four centuries on the land of Tennessee, a common element of exploration and enterprise. The motivating forces behind them have varied greatly from each to the next. Some were nationalistic in nature, some ethnic, some cultural; others were political, or social, or religious, or ideological; still others have been economic or commercial. The history of every state and every country is, at least in part, a running account of the endless succession of individuals who have merged their common interests and objectives in order to start anew, to form new alliances and build new communities. Human nature being what it is, the impulses have not always been pure; the desire to exploit and control and gain advantage has dominated almost as often as the desire to find liberty and equality and peace. Yet for good and ill, these new communities have added much to the total character and the history of Tennessee. Each has attempted in its own way to preserve a familiar way of life, to extend it from one setting to another, and, overall, the contribution they have made to the state's heritage has been positive and substantial.

There has been another group of new communities in Tennessee history that can be considered in a class apart from the ones already mentioned here. Rather than attempting to preserve and extend an accepted pattern of living, they were consciously founded on one theory or another of social reorganization, and their intent was not to recreate an image of the past but to give substance to an idealistic vision of the future. In a book he wrote in 1516, Thomas More described an imaginary island that had a perfect political and social system. He called the island—and his book—Utopia, and the word has survived as a descriptive term for the still-sought and still-imaginary social order that can justly be called ideal and perfect. A few of Tennessee's new communities seem legitimately to belong to the mixture of myth and reality and idealism that sets apart the utopias of history.

The most recent Tennessee utopian venture, and the only one currently in existence, is The Farm, a self-styled "family monastery" near Summertown in Lewis County. Established in 1970 by a former California college instructor named Stephen Gaskin, The Farm is a spiritual and agricultural commune embracing more than 1,500 acres of woods and fields and more than 800 people, most of them young adults and children. Having overcome the initial suspicions of their neighbors in the surrounding countryside, Gaskin and his followers have established themselves as a respected fixture on the local scene, even though their way of living differs greatly in many respects from that of the indigenous people. (Gaskin, with three of his disciples, served a prison sentence in 1974 for growing marijuana.) His spiritual teachings to his flock are a cosmopolitan blend of Eastern and Western religious thought, often couched in the contemporary vernacular of the American youth culture. The residents of The Farm hold all their property in common, eat no meat or dairy products, practice neither birth control nor abortion, and apparently regard Gaskin as a sort of messiah whose wisdom and leadership approach infallibility. That such beliefs and practices can coexist peacefully with the conservative traditions of people in rural Middle Tennessee seems surprising. On the other hand, the young residents of the commune are themselves conservative in many ways. In appearance, they resemble nineteenth-century country folks: they wear beards, long hair, bib overalls, full-length dresses and bonnets. They are industrious, hard-working, law-abiding, and—in their own fashion—pious, moralistic, and orthodox. And, in a county that had only 6,761 people in the 1970 census, The Farm represents a bloc vote that compels local politicians and officeholders to regard the colony with seriousness and respect.

One of the common characteristics of utopias is their impermanence. If The Farm follows the pattern of history, one of two things can be expected eventually to happen to it: it will become more and more like its surroundings (and thus no longer a utopia, a "perfect social order"), or it will break up and disappear. It is the faith of Gaskin and the people of The Farm that they have found the formula for a perfect social system, and that with it they can save the world. Such has been the faith of all utopians.

Gaskin's spiritual ancestor in Tennessee could be said to be Christian Gottlieb Priber, a German socialist and utopian who joined the Cherokee Nation in 1736 and for seven years labored to create what he called the "Kingdom of Paradise." Verner W. Crane wrote about him in a 1919 article in the *Sewanee Review*.

Priber was known as a polite, refined, well-educated, and intelligent man who believed deeply in equalitarianism and an open society. Such views were incompatible with the political and social thought of the times, and the price he paid for holding them was repeated exile, first from Germany, then from England, and finally, in 1735, from South Carolina. At Great Tellico, the principal town of the Overhill Cherokees, Priber became a willing and welcome convert among the Indian people, and there he lived until 1743, when he was captured and imprisoned by the British.

East Tennessee in those years was Cherokee land coveted by both the British and the French—those two forces of imperialism were soon to engage in a war for supremacy in the American wilderness—and each side suspected that Priber was an agent of the other. In fact, his loyalty was to neither, but to the Cherokees, whom he sought to protect from exploitation, and who in turn protected him from the Europeans who wanted him removed. Priber's idealistic conception of a Kingdom of Paradise envisioned a society in which "all colours and complexions" of people would live in friendship as equals, holding all things—including their children—in common. He also hoped to unite all Southern Indians into a single political body, and the French and English viewed such a "red empire" with alarm. The English, who were eventually to win the wilderness war, were particularly distrustful of Priber, and James Adair, one of the few Englishmen to see and talk to the elusive utopian during his years at Great Tellico, reported that Priber "impressed them [the Cherokees] with a very ill opinion of the English, representing them as a fraudulent, avaritious [sic], and encroaching people."

The Kingdom of Paradise apparently was well received by the Cherokees, who regarded Priber as an honored brother, but it had not reached an advanced state when he was finally seized and imprisoned for life. Priber was known to have in his possession when he was captured a dictionary of the Cherokee language and a manuscript describing his life among the Indians and his visionary plan for the Kingdom of Paradise. Both apparently were destroyed. The backwoods utopian died a few years later in a South Carolina prison. The Cherokees suffered under successive assaults from smallpox, from the British, and finally from the U. S. Government, which forced their removal to Oklahoma in 1838 on the infamous "Trail of Tears." The Kingdom of Paradise, and the Cherokee Nation itself, succumbed to what Christian Priber had called "an encroaching people."

Between the Kingdom of Paradise in the eighteenth century and The Farm in the twentieth, three fascinating and extraordinary utopian colonies came and went in Tennessee: Nashoba, in Shelby County, in the 1820s; Rugby, in Morgan County, in the 1880s; and Ruskin, in Dickson County, in the 1890s. Each of them was widely known in its time, and each merits a contemporary recounting.

2. Nashoba:
Frances Wright's Experiment
In "Practical Equality"

Frances Wright D'Arusmont was fifty-seven years old when she died in Cincinnati in 1852. Alienated from her family and friends, dismissed by society as yesterday's radical, she lived out her last years in silent retirement, a lonely and reclusive woman grown old before her time.

Her unnoted departure was but the last irony in the remarkable life of a woman who had seemed always to be before her time. Beginning in 1818, Fanny Wright had propelled herself to prominence in the United States and Europe, and for almost twenty years she was an outspoken advocate of democracy, abolition, women's rights, and the working class. She was a beautiful and charming individual, a radical reformer, a brilliant and controversial public figure who alternately inspired and outraged a generation of Americans. And as suddenly as she had appeared in the charmed circles of power on two continents, she disappeared after two decades and receded into the quiet and seldom-searched corners of history. Biographies of her life have been written, but she remains an obscure figure in the shadows of nineteenth-century America. And even more obscure is the single most extraordinary and ambitious undertaking of her life: Nashoba, a pioneering interracial utopia in the dense forests of West Tennessee.

Nashoba was founded in 1825, and ended in failure less than five years later. While it existed, it was one of the first and one of the few experimental attempts to find an alternative to slavery, and of all the endeavors to that end prior to the Civil War, it may have been the most practical and the most promising. The reasons for its decline were many, but in retrospect, the fact of its failure can be recognized as an early and unheeded warning of the grim consequences of human slavery.

Radicalism seemed to run in the family of Frances Wright. Her mother was an English aristocrat, but her father, a well-to-do Scottish landowner and merchant, felt more sympathy for the common people than for the upper class: James Wright celebrated the American and French revolutions (he published and distributed Thomas Paine's *The Rights of Man* in Scotland) and was an advocate and supporter of government reforms.

Within three years after Frances was born in Dundee in 1795, both of her parents died. She and her sister Camilla, one year younger than she, were reared by relatives in England. They received a classical education in London, and from an early age Frances in particular seemed destined to stand out among her peers. In personality and philosophy she was much like her liberal father. She became fluent in French and Italian, studied the Greek philosophers (Epicurus was her favorite), and spoke and wrote with informed and articulate self-assurance. One of her biographers said she had "a mind more quick than penetrating, more inquisitive than sagacious." She developed an acutely sensitive social conscience, a dislike of pretension, and a passion for reform. And, with that, she was also beautiful—a tall, slender, blue-eyed and auburn-haired young woman who could not fail to make a lasting impression wherever she went. Camilla was less dazzling, both intellectually and physically, and ordinarily deferred to her illustrious sister, but the two were very close from childhood on.

With the substantial inheritance they received from their father, the Wright sisters reached womanhood with a measure of independence and self-sufficiency uncommon for the times. The United States, that brash and boisterous new nation, attracted them irresistibly, and in 1818 they went to see it for themselves. Frances had written a play, *Altorf* ("a tale of freedom"), and saw it produced on a New York stage by a company of English actors. The two unaccompanied young ladies traveled freely about the country on what one scandalized observer called "a fool-hardy adventure," and they were as impressed with what they saw as most of the people they met were enchanted by them. America was to them an antidote to pessimism and was therefore the hope of the world, a virile new land of freedom which they saw as orderly and united, in contrast to England's "beggary, injustice, political and religious hypocrisy." The English novelist Anthony Trollope, whose mother was a close friend of the Wrights, spoke in later years of the remarkable Fanny, "very handsome in a large and almost masculine style of beauty with a most commanding presence, a superb figure, and noble features." She was, he said, a woman of "high-minded idealism, unselfishness, bravery, generosity. She had a fine and large intelligence, but not fine or large enough for going quite unpiloted across country." The woman Trollope described was not the

Matthew Rhea's famous 1832 map of Tennessee (top) showed Nashoba as a place name near the location of present-day Germantown. A drawing of Nashoba (bottom) was made in 1828 by French artist Auguste Hervieu, a friend of Frances Wright who visited the settlement.

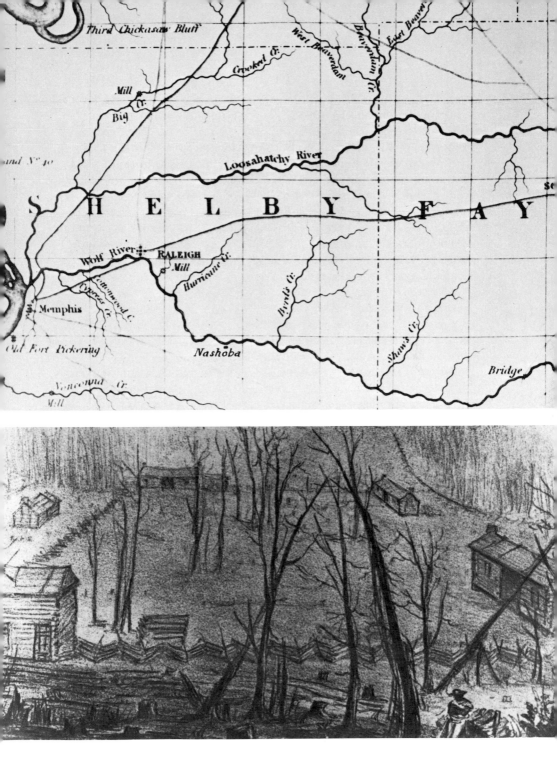

twenty-three-year-old Frances Wright on her first trip to America, but the mature and magnetic Fanny of the 1820s. It is not difficult to imagine, then, the sensation Fanny and Camilla caused on that first trip abroad.

Back in England in 1820, Fanny wrote a book about her travels—*Views on Society and Manners in America*—and it was published in several languages and won the acclaim of liberals and radicals all over Europe, as well as in the United States. It was a book, said one critic, "full of her prejudices and enthusiasms," and it described a nation unblemished except for one flaw: slavery. She had seen little of it at first hand, but enough to observe that it was an evil that should be ended, and although she did not say how that should be accomplished, she noted that the few free Negroes she had seen appeared in some respects to be worse off than slaves.

When the book came out, Frances Wright had already gained an impressive following. Thomas Jefferson had written to her in praise of her play after its presentation in New York, and Henry Clay quoted her in a speech in the House of Representatives. The noted English philosopher Jeremy Bentham, then past seventy but still active and influential, invited her to join his circle of intellectuals. But of all the men who applauded her, none was more important or more lavish in his praise than the Marquis de Lafayette, the famous general, hero of the American Revolution and honored citizen of France. He was living in retirement at La Grange, the family chateau outside Paris, and after he read Fanny's book he wrote to compliment her and to invite her for a visit. In September of 1821, she went.

Fanny Wright was then twenty-six years old, and Lafayette was sixty-four. He was a widower, but his children and grandchildren—and a steady stream of admirers and important visitors—kept his palatial home alive with activity, and the general, who still had a passion for political liberty and an ardent admiration for the United States, was the center of attention. Fanny came into the great man's presence impressed but unawed; Lafayette, who in his old age liked young women, was smitten. Here was a captivating and intelligent woman who shared his love for America and his distaste for slavery (Lafayette had emancipated the slaves on a plantation he owned in French Guiana before the French Revolution). What was more, this attractive lady whose father had died when she was a child seemed drawn to older men.

That was the beginning of an extraordinary friendship that lasted until the general died in 1834. For all intents and purposes, Fanny became a resident of La Grange. She was his secretary, his confidante, his biographer, and in all likelihood his lover, though on that point her biographers—and his—are discreetly silent. Fanny later said that she had his most intimate private and political confidence, and she urged him to adopt her—and Camilla, who also moved in—as his daughter (his children strenuously objected to that, and it was not done). Without question, this was to be the deepest emotional relationship of Fanny's life, more by far than a passing love affair. Clearly, she loved him very much; and, for his part, she was "my beloved, my adored Fanny, sweet child of my choice."

Lafayette had private quarters in one of the five massive towers of the chateau, and Fanny lived directly beneath his library and study. She spent long hours alone with him, handling his correspondence, writing his biography (she never finished it), and sharing in his still-active political intrigues. The blithe spirit who had come to dinner stayed for three years.

Lafayette's political power was by then on the wane, he was in financial straits, and his family was plainly embarrassed by his relationship with Fanny. They had, she said, "little minds and petty jealousies," and she surmised to Camilla that the general was forbidden to adopt them "by silly and ill-natured women who supposed intentions of another nature and the Lord knows what." When President James Monroe invited Lafayette to be feted by his American admirers, he readily accepted—and when Fanny announced she was going with him, the family once again was outraged.

Undaunted, she boarded the next ship after his, with Camilla at her side, and soon after they landed, they joined his entourage. The general was delighted, and the gossipmongers had a field day talking about the old man and his two beautiful young friends. They appeared with him at many balls and public functions in his honor, and shared with him the company of America's leading political figures—Monroe, James Madison, John Quincy Adams, Sam Houston, Andrew Jackson, and the aging Mr. Jefferson, then past eighty but busily engaged in the building of the University of Virginia. At Monticello, Lafayette introduced the Wright sisters to Jefferson (more precisely, presented them; they needed no introduction) as his adopted daughters who had been with him and his family for the past three years.

Frances Wright's reputation suffered from public perceptions of her behavior as eccentric at best, and at worst scandalous. She made no effort to combat such views; in fact, she never hesitated to do whatever she wanted to do, regardless of convention. The men she met seemed utterly charmed by her intelligence, her beauty, and her confidence, while their ladies were dismayed by her daring. But Fanny was no mere femme fatale; she was an imposing individual, a well-informed and serious-minded person with strong convictions and convincing sincerity. One writer has said of her that "her low, coarse voice commanded attention, and her good sense held it." Her friend Frances Trollope once called her "the most interesting woman in Europe," and remarked on "the splendor, the brilliance, the overwhelming eloquence, the wonderful power of her rich and thrilling voice." Furthermore, her compassion for the poor was genuine and deep-rooted. She was, according to a later assessment of her, "a sincere, great-hearted woman torn by the injustice and inequalities of life, eager to put an end to the sufferings of mankind." She thought of herself as a reformer but not a radical, an idealist but also a pragmatist. And as she traveled about the country with Lafayette, she came inevitably to the conclusion that slavery, the wart on America's rosy cheek, had to be removed.

On the estates of Jefferson and Madison in Virginia, she saw slavery practiced by otherwise liberal men, and heard them speak about it apologetically. They acknowledged that it was a dreadful calamity, but said they could find no way to end it. Fanny was disturbed by the chasm that divided the ideal of freedom from the reality of slavery, and by the general acceptance of it. The foreign slave trade had been outlawed in 1808, and slavery was unlawful in all but those states that were economically dependent upon it. It was in many respects an involuntary system, not only for the blacks who suffered under it but also for many farmers who owned them. Manumission was widely discussed, and in several Southern state legislatures, including Tennessee's, laws calling for the freeing of all slaves had been introduced. But the counter argument always prevailed; the fear of economic and social disaster tightened the grip of the slavery advocates.

In her book about America, Frances Wright had described the effort of Edward Coles, an abolitionist, to prepare seventeen ex-slaves for self-sufficiency on a farm in southern Illinois, and her optimistic conclusion was that in the near future, there would be no more slavery in the United States. On her return trip, however, she saw for the first time a vessel loaded with chained black people bound for New Orleans, saw that slavery was still flourishing, and knew that her optimism had been premature. Abolitionists were calling for immediate freedom for all slaves; the advocates of slavery were vowing never to abandon the practice and were trying to spread it to other states; and the masses of people seemed to be somewhere between those two positions. That silent majority dividing the radicals from the reactionaries was the group Fanny wanted to influence. As ardently as she opposed slavery, she felt that sudden emancipation would not result in real freedom for the blacks because, in the wretched circumstances under which they lived, they were not prepared for self-sufficiency. Believing that most American whites would gladly accept a plan of gradual abolition that did not cause them financial ruin, she began to fashion such a plan.

Of uncertain origin is this painting of "Frances Wright at 32 in the costume adopted by the New Harmony Community in 1826." It appears without credit in a biography of the founder of Nashoba written in the 1930s by Alice J. Perkins and Theresa Wolfson.

In the summer of 1825, she put before Lafayette her proposal to buy a small number of slaves without loss to their owners, and set up a colony where they could be trained to be self-supporting and prepared for freedom. Jefferson, Madison, Monroe, and others also reviewed it, and all of them gave their enthusiastic approval. Fanny asked Jefferson to take an active part in the venture; he declined, citing his age and his university duties, but he was warmly encouraging and wished her well. Lafayette, who was preparing to return to France, put her in touch with Andrew Jackson, the war hero who soon would be President, and at Jackson's invitation, she went to Tennessee to seek a site for her colony.

Fanny's vision was to form a community in which whites and blacks, working together, could educate and elevate the former slaves to full equality and freedom, in the hope that their example would hasten the abolition of all slavery. The more radical of the abolitionists, she felt, had "much zeal but little knowledge." The reactionary defenders of slavery, on the other hand, were perpetuating "a sin against humanity" and threatening the survival of the new nation. Fanny sought a middle solution, a way to assure freedom and independence for blacks and to allow the agricultural South to find another base for its economy. If slaves could be freed without loss to their owners, she reasoned, it would be a double gain for society. Her plan was to buy land in a Southern state, acquire a number of slaves by gift or purchase, charge each individual the amount of his purchase price, apply his work in the colony to the payment of his debt, and eventually resettle the former slaves in a colony outside the United States. She estimated that the cycle would take five years to complete, and her plan included schooling and industrial training, special care for children, and a careful effort to keep families together.

The particulars of that plan seem puzzling now, even contradictory. The slaves whose freedom she proposed to purchase would actually remain slaves until they worked out their freedom, and once they had done that, they would be sent out of the country to establish their own segregated society. Further, the intent to hold families together seems incompatible with the plan for children, which involved raising from infancy a generation of educated, self-reliant people free of degradation and inferiority. Obviously, that could not be done in a five-year cycle. And finally, the kind of freedom and equality resulting from such a plan could hardly be called that: it would more likely be a form of benevolent paternalism and dependency.

Those contradictions, and others then unforeseen, were destined to surface later. In the context of the times, they could not have been fully grasped. Frances Wright had good intentions, and her plan was, relatively speaking, moderate and practical. She went to visit the Rappite colonies in Pennsylvania and Indiana, and met Robert Owen, a fellow Scot, and was inspired by his new cooperative community at New Harmony, Indiana. And then, with $12,000 of her own money, she rode on horseback from Virginia to Tennessee with George Flower, a young emancipationist and friend of Lafayette's, arriving in Nashville in September 1825. With the assistance of Andrew Jackson, they journeyed on to Memphis to meet John Overton, a friend and business associate of Jackson's, and there, in October, Fanny bought the first 300 acres of what was to become a 2,000-acre estate. The price was nine cents an acre.

Memphis at that time was little more than a fur trading station and military outpost, and only a handful of permanent settlers had cleared land and built cabins there. The Chickasaws, under heavy pressure from the wave of whites moving west, had sold what is now western Kentucky and Tennessee to the United States in 1818. Shelby County was established the following year and a town was laid out on the river, but it was not until 1826 that Memphis was actually incorporated, with a population of about 500. John Overton and James Winchester, another close associate of Jackson, jointly controlled large tracts of land in the area, and it was Overton and some of his colleagues who made available the acreage Fanny Wright bought along the Wolf River, a dozen or more miles east of the Memphis settlement on the Mississippi. The Chickasaw word for the Wolf was Nashoba, and Fanny gave that name to what she intended to be her colony.

The first mayor of Memphis was James Winchester's son Marcus, a handsome and adventurous young man whose wife was a dark-skinned Creole woman from New Orleans. The Winchesters and James Richardson, a young Scotsman, soon became Fanny's friends and supporters, as did a man named Richeson Whitby. George Flower went back to Illinois to get his family—and Camilla, who was staying with them. Fanny, after making arrangements to buy several slaves in Nashville, spent the winter with her new friends in Memphis, planning the development of her new estate.

It must have been an exciting time for her. She was on the threshold of a grand and idealistic experiment that had already attracted an inordinate amount of attention wherever it was known. Even her disapproving critics had to be impressed with this thirty-year-old woman who had given up the ease and elegance of a lofty social circle to devote herself to a life of sacrifice and service in the wilderness. Her admirers talked in wonderment of the tall, splendid-looking woman whose dark curls were cut short in defiance of convention, who dressed indifferently and walked with the long stride of a man, who traded with the Indians and made long journeys alone on horseback and showed no fear of bears and wolves in the woods. In the late winter of

1826, when Flower and his family returned with Camilla, they found Fanny exuberant and eager to begin work. The slaves she had bought were brought down from Nashville, and with the first sign of spring, the colony was formally launched.

The first white residents were Fanny, Camilla, Flower and his wife and three children, James Richardson, and Richeson Whitby, who had come from New Harmony. The black contingent included eight or ten men and women from Nashville, purchased at an average price of $450 each, and a mother and her six daughters, given to Fanny by a South Carolina planter (the father of the girls perhaps) who wanted them freed. Working together, they set out first to build two large cabins and clear about fifteen acres of land, and the magnitude of that task quickly took its toll. What began in the gray chill of departing winter continued without ceasing in the oppressive and malarial heat of summer. Flower's children became ill, and he took his family back to the North. Fanny had been writing glowing letters about her Eden to friends in Europe, but she was in fact becoming feverish and exhausted herself, and in late summer she departed for New Harmony to recover her strength, leaving Richardson, Whitby, and Camilla to carry on the work.

The difficulties at Nashoba in its first year of existence derived not from opposition or hostility to the colony—indifference was more characteristic of the local reaction—but from the laborious and demanding work, the punishing climate, and the sobering realization that making a utopia is infinitely more complex than imagining one. Fanny remained at New Harmony until the spring of 1827, recuperating from her illness and pondering her next steps. Under the influence of Robert Owen, she began to revise and enlarge her plans for Nashoba.

The elevation of black slaves to self-sufficiency, she decided, was not enough; the colony should become an interracial cooperative village where all property would be held in common, formal religion would be discouraged as an enemy of liberalism and progress, and marriage would be not a binding legal contract but a free and informal agreement between willing partners. Whether those were her convictions or Owen's, it is hard to say. To be sure, she was highly critical of the church and regarded marriage as a trap for any intelligent woman, but those views had not been part of her vision of Nashoba until that winter 'at New Harmony. Before she returned to Tennessee, she created a board of trustees and conveyed to them all of the land and property of the colony. And to a friend in Europe she wrote: "I have devoted my time and fortune to laying the foundations of an establishment where affection shall form the only marriage, kind feelings and kind action the only religion, regard for the feelings and liberties of others the only restraint, and union of interests the bond of peace and security.'' The goal of freedom and equality for former slaves had been subsumed under a larger ideology.

Ironically, Owen's New Harmony community, which had been based on many of the same ideals, was in the process of disintegration by the time Frances Wright left, and Robert Dale Owen, the twenty-six-year-old son of the founder, went with her to Nashoba. There they found that about 100 acres of forest had been cleared and several cabins built, but there was much sickness, and little work in progress. Fanny herself was still far from healthy. Distressed that her dream of education and training had borne no fruit, she initiated weekly meetings to stimulate progress and inspire a "sense of individual responsibility.'' They had little effect. The confused slaves—they were still called that—heard stern rules and laws on one hand, and discourses about freedom on the other. Camilla and Whitby were in love, and neither they nor James Richardson were able to carry out Fanny's instructions—the ones she left with them when she went to New Harmony, or the ones she brought back with her. Both the whites and the blacks seemed unable to escape the master-slave reflex: the former were still domineering, the latter subservient. And to make matters worse, Fanny was running out of money.

In May 1827 she decided to go to Europe, for two reasons: to solicit more funds and support for Nashoba, and to recover from the persistent illness (probably dengue fever, or malaria) that had weakened her in body and spirit. Nashoba was then under the nominal control of the ten trustees she had named—the Owens (father and son), Whitby, Richardson, Flower, Camilla, the faithful General Lafayette, and three other men. Leaving Richardson, Whitby, and Camilla there as resident trustees, Fanny departed with Robert Dale Owen, and while waiting in New Orleans to embark for Europe, she engaged a free mulatto woman named Mam'selle Lolotte to go to Nashoba and establish a school.

Fanny was seriously ill—so ill that for a time the young Owen feared for her life—but after several days at sea she began to regain her strength, and when Owen left her with friends in Paris, she was almost fully recovered. Like so many others before him—and after—Owen was deeply affected by Fanny. He remarked later in his life that she "mainly shaped, for several years, the course and tenor of my life.'' Their relationship had been strictly platonic, he said, and his love for her was not blind: he observed that she had a high opinion of her own intelligence, and was stubborn, extravagant, immature, and naïve in many of her views. But she was, nevertheless, unforgettable.

The trip removed Fanny from all contact with Nashoba for more than two months, and before any news of the colony caught up with her, she was swept up in the pleasant and comfortable life she had once known. The old charm and magnetism returned, and she inspired her listeners with romantic accounts of her great experiment in America. She paid an extended visit to Lafayette at La Grange, to the old man's everlasting joy, and she persuaded Frances Trollope, her fond and long-time friend, to return with her to Tennessee. All in all, her reception in Europe was triumphant. Mrs. Trollope was to say of Fanny later that her overall appearance had a profound effect on others "unlike anything I have ever seen before or ever expect to see again."

But in her absence, Nashoba had slipped further into crisis and controversy. The trouble started within a week after her departure. Whitby and Richardson proved to be poor managers, and Camilla lacked her sister's vision as well as her judgment. A log of the community meetings gives some insight into what went wrong:

Sunday Evening, May 20, 1827

Camilla Wright and James Richardson, resident trustees. Met the slaves—Camilla Wright repeated to them how the work was to proceed. . . . She also informed them that to-morrow, the children, Delila, Lucy, Julia, and Alfred, will be taken altogether from under the management of the parents, and will be placed, until our school is organized, under the management of Mam'selle Lolotte; that all communication between the parents and children shall, in future, be prevented, except such as may take place by permission, and in the presence of the manager of the children. That Violet, one of Dilly's children, should be placed especially under the management of Josephine, the daughter of Mam'selle Lolotte.

May 24th

Two women slaves tied up and flogged by James Richardson in the presence of Camilla and all the slaves. Two dozen and one dozen on bare back with a cowskin.

Saturday Evening, May 26, 1827

Agreed, that the slaves shall not be allowed to receive money, clothing, food, or indeed anything whatever from any person resident at, or visiting this place . . . and, that any article so received, shall be returned to the giver in the presence of the slaves and trustees. . . . Agreed, that the slaves shall not be permitted to eat elsewhere than at the public meals, excepting in case of such sickness as may render confinement to their cabins necessary.

Sunday Evening, May 27, 1827

Met the slaves—Camilla Wright informed them of the regulations agreed to yesterday evening. Dilly having given utterance a day or two ago, to some grumbling at having so many mistresses, James Richardson stated to them, that it is very true they have many mistresses as well as many masters, and that in all probability, they will soon have many more of both; as every free person who shall reside here, whether black, white, or brown, will be, in some sort, their master or mistress; that this is just the difference between a free person and a slave; and that they can get rid of these masters and mistresses in no other way than by working out their freedom, when they will be transformed into masters and mistresses themselves, but that, in the meantime, they will gradually find out, that this multiplicity of superiors, so far from being a hardship, is of palpable advantage to them, in preventing them from being at the mercy of the temper of any one individual.

These abuses of the black residents of Nashoba were so contradictory of Frances Wright's public expressions of sympathy and concern for slaves that it is difficult to believe she could have approved. To put the children in the charge of a teacher was one thing; to cut them off from all communication with their parents was quite another. The floggings, the restrictions on receiving material goods and on eating, the assertion that all free persons are automatically the superiors of all former slaves—these seem such perversions of the spirit that led to the founding of Nashoba in the first place that Fanny must have shuddered when she heard of them.

But the treatment of the blacks, however much it may have disturbed Fanny, was not a cause of controversy around Nashoba. It was, on the contrary, standard procedure. The people of Memphis, when they heard such stories, could hardly have been alarmed to learn that their utopian neighbors handled blacks the same way they did. In fact, they may have been relieved by that news. It was what followed next that outraged Nashoba's white neighbors. Once again, the log tells the story:

Friday, June 1, 1827

Met the slaves at dinner time—Isabel had laid a complaint against Redrick, for coming during the night of Wednesday to her bedroom, uninvited, and endeavoring, without her consent, to take liberties with her person. Our views on the sexual relation had been repeatedly given to the slaves; Camilla Wright again stated it, and informed the slaves that, as the conduct of Redrick, which he did not deny, was a gross infringement of that view, a repetition of such conduct, by him, or by any other of the men, ought in her opinion, to be punished by flogging. She repeated that we consider the proper basis of the sexual intercourse to be the unconstrained and unrestrained choice of *both parties*. Nelly having requested a lock for the door of the room in which she and Isabel sleep, with the view of preventing the future uninvited entrance of any man, the lock was refused, as being, in its proposed use, inconsistent with the doctrine just explained; a doctrine which we are determined to enforce, and which will give to every woman a much greater security, than any lock can possibly do.

Sunday Evening, June 3, 1827

Met the slaves—Willis having, a few days ago, complained to Camilla Wright of Mam'selle Lolotte's children beating his children; thinking it was allowed because hers were a little the fairest. James Richardson took the opportunity of endeavoring to explain to the slaves, our views on the subject of color. He told them that, in our estimation all colors are equal in rank, and that whatever distinction may be established on this place, color shall form the basis of none of them.

Sunday Evening, June 17, 1827

Met the slaves—James Richardson informed them that, last night, Mam'selle Josephine and he began to live together; and he took this occasion of repeating to them our views on color, and on the sexual relation.

These accounts were published—apparently with Richardson's approval, if not encouragement—and a storm of indignation and hostility quickly followed. Nashoba was no brothel, he said; it was a community free of hypocrisy. He defended his behavior, and added further insult to injury by declaring that he was also an atheist. Camilla supported him, and so, presumably, did Whitby. To the surrounding society's three sacred institutions— marriage, religion, and white supremacy—the resident trustees of Nashoba had thus advocated three outrageous alternatives: free love, atheism, and amalgamation.

The colony was so beseiged with problems before Richardson's pronouncements that its future was already in doubt. In spite of its initial objective of attaining equality and freedom for former slaves, it had fostered an inferior status for blacks by keeping them in slavery and requiring them to do the hard work while whites did what they pleased. While proclaiming that all colors were equal, it nourished the distinction between slaves and freemen—and the slaves, being black, suffered that contradiction. The colony was on the brink of financial collapse, and it had been so mismanaged that it was nearly beyond recovery. It had attracted new residents—some with capital and some without, some who worked, others who boarded, still others who freeloaded—and inequality even among the whites was out of hand. What had been intended as an economically sound and feasible alternative to slavery was about to end as another bankrupt utopia. The published logs not only hastened its death; they also endangered the lives of its residents.

Fanny Wright's immediate reaction upon hearing of these developments is not clear, but most of the Nashoba trustees—excepting those on the scene—were shocked and dismayed, and they pleaded with Fanny to repudiate the excesses of Richardson, Whitby, and Camilla. Her friends in Europe were even less understanding; only Frances Trollope stood by her. Late in 1827, she went to Mrs. Trollope's home in England and prepared her response to the seething controversy. It was published without comment in a Memphis newspaper in January 1828, while the two women were at sea on the journey back to Nashoba.

Fanny was never one to duck a fight. Ignoring the advice of her friends, she wrote a defense of the resident trustees that was in many ways as inflammatory as their actions had been. She not only confirmed the published reports; she sanctioned them, and for good measure attacked the "tyranny of matrimonial law which had its foundation in religious prejudice." The United States, she charged, offered its people political liberty but not moral liberty, and she asked rhetorically: "Liberty without equality, what is it but a chimera?" Henceforth, she asserted, Nashoba would be a cooperative community where whites and free blacks would live and work together while their children were educated in common as equals. By implication, she seemed to be supporting an even stronger interracial bond in the colony than she had advocated in the beginning—and certainly a more equitable relationship than Richardson and the others had in fact practiced.

When Fanny and Mrs. Trollope arrived at Nashoba, Camilla and Whitby were legally married and Richardson and Mam'selle Lolotte's daughter Josephine were gone. Those two developments had the effect of releasing the pressure of community indignation, and with the passage of a little time, the colony had become relatively tranquil. Mrs. Trollope, however, did not find it so. She was appalled by "the savage aspect of the scene." What Fanny had called her Eden could only be seen by the proper Englishwoman as primitive, desolate, rude, and unhealthy. "One glance sufficed to convince me," she wrote later, "that every idea I had formed of the place was as far as possible from the truth." She had three of her children with her, and after abiding the "miserable and melancholy mode of living" for ten days, she bundled them up and took a boat upriver to Cincinnati. Fanny, she said, was as devoted as a religious fanatic, and as blind to reality. It was the end of their friendship. Mrs. Trollope saw Camilla again, but ever after feared association with the notorious Fanny.

For six months, Fanny stayed on in a game struggle to salvage something from Nashoba. Whitby and Camilla were still there, and Robert Dale Owen came back briefly, but they were, by one account, "desperate people trying to keep a crumbling society together." The idealistic dream of a new community was gone; all that remained was a loose association of individuals. Whitby was in failing health. He and Camilla left, and Owen went back to New Harmony. In June 1828 Fanny followed him. About thirty blacks remained, their rights unrealized, their status unclear, their future in doubt. Practically speaking, Nashoba was finished.

For the next several months, Fanny and the younger Owen edited a newspaper they called the *New Harmony and Nashoba Gazette*. They had crossed back over the thin and indistinct line that separates activism from advocacy, and only once again was Fanny to attempt a practical demonstration of her radical ideas. "She had the eyes of a philosopher, not an abolitionist," someone once said of her, and as a writer and lecturer she went on to more notoriety, exhorting reforms but not organizing them. The *Gazette* was the beginning. First in New Harmony and later in New York (as the *Free Inquirer*), it stridently attacked slavery, organized religion, marriage, and the monied class, and advocated social and political equality for blacks and women, universal public education, labor unions, religious freedom, and what in today's terminology would be called open marriage and no-fault divorce. Fanny also lectured against capital punishment and imprisonment for debt, and spoke out for separation of church and state, temperance, freedom of speech, and birth control. By one account, she was the first woman to lecture on politics from a public platform, and by all accounts she was one of the earliest and most outspoken champions of women's rights. "Fanny Wright had ideas out of step with her time in history," said one writer of her, in an understatement of classic proportions, and he added: "She would have been too much for the public to accept if she had lived a century later."

In 1829 Fanny moved to New York with Owen and bought an old church, which they called their "hall of science," a headquarters for their lecturing and publishing ventures and for a brief and abortive attempt at political activity. With two others, they formed the Workingmen's Party, but it was short-lived. Camilla, meanwhile, had left Whitby, and with their child she moved into the same house in New York where Fanny and Owen were living with another former New Harmony resident, a Frenchman named William Phiquepal D'Arusmont.

Absorbed as she was in her widening crusade for social reforms, Fanny could not shake Nashoba from her mind. All that it had been—or might have been—had collapsed under the inconsistencies and indiscretions of the people she had left in charge. She had defended them, and taken the brunt of public

THE NEW-HARMONY AND NASHOBA GAZETTE,

SECOND SERIES.
VOL. 1.—NO. 8.
Published every Wednesday.

OR

THE FREE ENQUIRER.

WHOLE SERIES.
VOL. 4.—NO. 164.
Terms: $3 per ann. in adv

JUST OPINIONS ARE THE RESULT OF JUST KNOWLEDGE.—JUST PRACTICE OF JUST OPINIONS.

NEW-HARMONY, (IND.) WEDNESDAY, DECEMBER 17, 1828.

NOTES
FROM MY POCKET BOOK.

I.

I know not if much learning "make men mad," as the Roman Governor is said to have told Paul; but it most assuredly makes very many foolish. How many weak heads are there that would never have been heard of, had they not been crammed with Greek, Latin, false logic and long words, in those nurseries of error called Schools and Colleges! In the actual state of human knowledge, learning, so called, is an admirable second, but a sorry principal.

II.

It is probable that a shrewd peasant could more easily confound a philosopher, than one of his own fraternity; and a savage, stagger a holy believer, rather than a logician. When a Christian Missionary related to a party of Indians his story of the Creation and the fall of man, an old Chief replied with the simplicity of unsophisticated reason: "It seems to me, father, that your God loved his apples very much, and his children very little." How, after this simple apostrophe, might the convertor of souls return to the charge?

This recalls to me, that, when barely seven years of age, I observed to a good old lady, who had charged herself with my instruction in the elements of things sacred and profane: "You have told me a great deal about God's son; but you have never told me any thing about God's wife." "And pray do you remember what you replied?" I asked of my old friend, when, ten years afterwards, she recalled to me the anecdote. "Why—I believe I was at a non-plus." F. W.

A PARISIAN ANECDOTE.

There is perhaps scarcely any class in any country, where instances of more genuine liberality of sentiment, and of greater freedom from ignorant prejudice are to be found, than among the members of the liberal professions in Paris; particularly among physicians.

During a meeting of the Parisian faculty of Physicians in the hall of the College of Medecine, a gentleman happened to be present who had just returned from a visit to the United States, where he had passed several years. In the course of conversation the sect of Quakers was mentioned, whose doctrines and peculiarities are little known in Paris, as few of its members ever visit the French metropolis. Mr. Lallemand first surgeon to the Hospital *de la Salpêtrière*, and one of the most justly distinguished members of the College and of his profession, turned to the traveller. "Monsieur P—," said he, "has resided in the United States; he can doubtless give us some information regarding this strange sect." The gentleman mentioned several of the peculiarities that characterize the Society of Friends; and among others, "that they had neither priest, lawyer nor soldier in their society."

"Have they any physicians?" asked Lallemand, with playful eagerness.

"Yes."

"Ah!" replied the physician, shaking his head with good-humored *naïveté*, "*ils ne sont sages, donc, qu'à trois quarts!*"* R. D. O.

RELIGION AND INSANITY.

The following are extracts from a Review of a recent publication, taken from a London Journal for September last.

Commentaries on the Causes, Forms, Symptoms, and Treatments, Moral and Medical, of Insanity. By G. Man Burrows, M. D., &c. 8vo. pp. 716. London, 1828.

This elaborate treatise, the fruit of much observation and great experience, is a work of the utmost medical and general importance. Addressed to the investigation of a class of maladies which are, we fear, becoming more and more prevalent, Dr. Burrows produces an immense number of cases on which his acute reasoning is founded, and traces insanity, in all its forms of mania, melancholia, demency, idiocy, &c. to the various moral and physical causes which produce that almost worst of human afflictions. Having exhibited the evil, and explained the diseases complicated with or consequent upon it, the author ably points out the best modes of treating the unhappy sufferers; and, in short, gives us a complete view of the origins, the appearances, and the remedies (where cures are possible) of the distressing cases which rank under the common name of insanity.

In perusing this volume, a mass of the most extraordinary instances of madness arising out of singular circumstances will be found: they seem to be horrid sports of a demon Power, which, whether it obtains a means in nerve, or blood, or brain, or any other portion of the bodily frame, works its dreadful and mysterious effects, prostrating the noblest intellects, and debasing or destroying the finest faculties of mind. Is it not wonderful that the apprehension so like that of a God should be utterly overthrown by some slight tumor, or either the too quick momentum or stoppage of an inconsiderable fluid through a small vessel or

* They are but three-fourths wise, then,

extreme limb? And the moral causes are not less strange: among them, religion operates widely, and we will illustrate the book by an extract referring to this interesting branch of the enquiry. *   *   *   *

"Dr. Hallaran, who has had the best opportunities for observation, remarks, that in the Cork Lunatic Asylum, where Catholics are in proportion to Protestants as ten to one, no instance has occurred of mental derangement among the former from religious enthusiasm; but several dissenters from the established church have been so affected. The reason of this difference appears obvious. The ministers of the Romish persuasion will not permit their flocks to be wrought upon. To distrust the fallibility of any point of doctrine or discipline, is with them heresy. Catholics, therefore, are preserved from those dubitations, which, when once engendered, generally end in conversion. The moment of danger is, when ancient opinions in matters of faith are wavering, or in the novitiate of those recently embraced. And to this danger every Protestant is more particularly exposed, especially in a country where toleration in religious opinions is allowed; for there, excess of fervor is the most likely to be awakened. Enthusiasm and insanity bear such close affinity, that the shades are often too indistinct to define which is one and which the other. Exuberance of zeal on any subject, in some constitutions, soon ripens into madness: but excess of religious enthusiasm, unless tempered by an habitual command over the affective passions, usually and readily degenerates into fanaticism; thence to superstition the transition is in sequence; and permanent delirium too often closes the scene. Enthusiasm and superstition, however, are not necessarily in sequence; for they are as opposite in character as, generally, in effect. The one is almost always the concomitant of genius or a vigorous mind, and may inspire the purest piety or benevolence, or emulate deeds of the highest glory; while the other seldom invades genius, except when extenuated by some corporeal disorder; but is commonly confined to the weak, the timid, and the uninformed; and in them produces either the blindest fury or the most gloomy despondency, and sometimes the wildest schemes for propitiating the offended Deity." *   *   *

Examples.—"A gentleman of fortune and some consideration, but who had become highly nervous, and somewhat hipochondrical and gloomy, anxious that his son should be educated with strict principles of religion, placed him under the care of several divines in succession, each of whom was enjoined to be very attentive to his religious instruction.

Frances Wright initialed these "Notes From My Pocket Book" in a December 1828 edition of The New-Harmony and Nashoba Gazette, *a paper she edited for a brief time with Robert Dale Owen. The following year, she and Owen moved the enterprise to New York, calling it* The Free Enquirer.

outrage on herself, and in the aftermath, the failure of Nashoba nagged at her conscience.

So in December of 1829 she went back. Thirty-one black residents were still there, their condition essentially unchanged from eighteen months earlier, when Fanny had last seen them. She told them she had come to the conclusion that color was, in fact, a barrier to equality in America, and she saw no prospect that any of them would ever be able to gain freedom and independence and equity in a land of slavery and white supremacy. She proposed to take them to Haiti, where they could live as free people in a black-ruled nation, and they agreed to go. In January 1830, accompanied by Phiquepal D'Arusmont, she sailed from New Orleans on the *John Quincy Adams,* a chartered brig, with the entire black population of Nashoba— thirteen adults and eighteen children. By the time they arrived, Haiti's president, Jean Pierre Boyer, had received a warm letter from the ever-helpful Lafayette, introducing Fanny and commending her plan of emancipation. Boyer promised the blacks land and jobs, and presented Fanny with a shipment of coffee to repay the cost of the chartered ship in New Orleans. Almost exactly four years after its formal beginning, Frances Wright's celebrated emancipationist experiment in the Tennessee wilderness came to its formal ending on the soil of a black nation in the Caribbean. The long-suffering blacks of Nashoba were free at last.

"For the first time," Fanny wrote later, "I bowed my head in humility before the omnipotence of collective humanity." Nashoba had cost her many thousands of dollars, a multitude of friends, and much personal anguish. If it had ended well for the thirty-one blacks, it was for Fanny the first crippling defeat of her life. And it would not be the last.

A New York newspaper, the *Commercial Advertiser,* printed an account of the Haitian journey, asserting that the blacks she escorted there were not slaves but free blacks she had paid to make the trip. Furthermore, the paper said, Fanny had received 100 gold doubloons from Haiti's president "for familiarities she had engaged in." Fanny demanded a retraction from the publisher and got it. It was the only slander she ever took the trouble to refute.

But her notoriety continued. She was called "the priestess of infidelity," a "Godless and immoral woman," a "free thinker and a free lover." James Madison wrote to Lafayette complaining of her behavior, and the general was sympathetic; he too was dismayed. She was an unrestrained free spirit, envied and hated but never ignored. And she was also weary, dispirited, and unhappy. Camilla's child became ill and died, and at about the same time, Fanny learned that she was pregnant, presumably by "the eccentric little French physician," D'Arusmont, who was sixteen years her senior. He returned to

France, and late in 1830, the Wright sisters also went to Paris. Early the next year, Fanny married D'Arusmont—a paradoxical turnabout for the woman who had so roundly denounced marriage—and Lafayette stood with her once more, as a witness to the event. Her child was born, but died in infancy, and then Camilla, her beloved sister and lifelong companion, also died.

For the next four years, Fanny lived a quiet life out of the limelight in Paris. In 1832 she gave birth to a daughter, Frances Sylva D'Arusmont, and though she apparently did not love her husband, they lived comfortably and compatibly for a time. But Fanny was not the same. Gone were "her eloquence and mischief, her wisdom and folly." Friends remarked of her "dry, cold, dictatorial manner." Her old friend Lafayette, the venerable warrior, passed away in 1834, and with him went her last happy connection with the past.

As she grew more and more restless, Fanny began to travel again, first in France, then England, and finally, in 1835, back in the United States. Altogether, she made several more trips to America, dabbling in politics and a variety of causes, and on most of those journeys her husband stayed at home with their child. She was a convincing supporter of President Andrew Jackson, her old friend—whether to his delight or dismay, it is impossible to say—and undoubtedly she saw Robert Dale Owen again, possibly during the years between 1843 and 1847, when he was a congressman from Indiana. Nashoba had been returned to her by its trustees, and she went there several times. A Memphis newspaper described her on one of those visits as "a hale, buxom 'grass widow'"—by which it could have meant a separated or divorced woman, a discarded mistress, or an unmarried mother, none of which she was, but all of which she came close to being. On a later trip to Memphis, in the late 1840s, she filed for divorce. D'Arusmont wrote her: "Your life was essentially an external life. You loved virtue deeply, but you loved also, and perhaps even more, grandeur and glory." Their daughter Sylva, by then a teenager, stayed with her father.

Fanny moved to Cincinnati. In 1852, she suffered a broken hip in a fall from a carriage, and the once-elegant woman who had stood five feet ten inches tall in her prime was a stooped and crippled shadow of her former self. That same year she died, very much alone and a figure of the past—yet only fifty-seven years old. In her will, she left all of her possessions, including the Nashoba property, to her twenty-year-old daughter, "who has been alienated from me, but to whom I give my blessing and forgiveness."

The ultimate irony of Frances Wright's life is that she died a forgotten figure, for she had been, to friend and enemy alike, a truly unforgettable woman. She was a splendid paradox—generous and selfish, tough and tender, wise and foolish. Even the dictionaries of biography are ambivalent about her: one calls her a "philanthropist and agitator," another describes her as "benevolent, unselfish, eccentric and fearless." She had an abundance of critics. One said she suffered from a "sclerosis of temperament which often goes with humanitarian activities," that she became a humanitarian and lost her humanity. Another, more generous, concluded that she was guilty of "much miscalculation, but no fanaticism. Her errors sprang from the weaknesses of a generous mind. Had she stuck to abolition as her one cause, she might have had more impact."

One of the last in the long and impressive line of famous men who admired her was Walt Whitman, who must have met Fanny in the 1840s, when he was a young school teacher and journalist in New York. "She was a brilliant woman of beauty," he later recalled, "who was never satisfied unless she was busy doing good. . . . beautiful in bodily shape and gifts of soul. We all loved her, fell down before her, her very appearance seemed to enthrall. . . . I never felt so glowingly towards any other woman."

Finally, the last word to say who Fanny Wright was and what she aspired to be properly belongs to her. In her lectures, published by the *Free Enquirer* in 1831, she described herself as a reformer but not a radical, and a seeker after equality in all things. What she wanted, she said, was "practical equality . . . universal and equal improvement of the condition of all, until . . . the American people shall present, in another generation, but one class, and, as it were, but one family. . . . Each independent in his and her own thoughts, actions, rights, possessions, and all cooperating to promote the common weal."

The story of Frances Wright and her Nashoba might have ended there, but it did not. It remained for her daughter to add a fascinating footnote that continued for another fifty years.

Sylva D'Arusmont, having lived her early years in France, had no first-hand knowledge of Nashoba, or of the United States at large. After her father died in 1855, she went to America to inspect her inheritance, and apparently decided the Nashoba property was worth keeping. Back in France, she persuaded a man named Eugene de Lagutery to enter a lease-purchase agreement with her under which he would take over the property and pay her a regular income in return. De Lagutery—who soon Americanized his name to Guthrie—moved with his family to Memphis, and hired a Cincinnati man to manage Nashoba and develop it into a resort. Some timber was cleared and a hotel was started in about 1860, but troubles were at hand. Guthrie's unhappy wife took two of their three daughters and went back to Paris, and Guthrie went to Cincinnati, where Sylva had moved in the meantime. The resident manager at Nashoba was left to settle things there as best he could, and the resort scheme was abandoned. Guthrie heard nothing from his wife, and then he said he learned in a French newspaper that she was dead. He and Sylva were married in about 1865.

On a later trip to Europe, they saw the first Mrs. Guthrie, very much alive, and that bizarre experience was followed by a succession of strange and confusing events, the chronology of which is far from clear in the available accounts. Guthrie and Sylva lived at her grandfather's old estate in Dundee, Scotland, long enough for her to have three children, the first of whom was born in 1868. The resident manager of Nashoba filed a court suit claiming the property as his own, and he was awarded title to the land. The first Mrs. Guthrie apparently did not challenge her husband's marriage to Sylva, but it is not clear how the resulting legal tangle was unsnarled. And finally, in 1873, Guthrie himself died in Italy, and Sylva, who had also lost one of her children, took her two small sons and returned that same year to the United States.

One of her first acts was to ask the court in Memphis to return to her the property she had inherited from her mother and then sold to her late husband. In a complex and involved legal struggle that lasted five years, Sylva was finally victorious. The court awarded her 1,422 acres in 1878, and she moved into the old manor house that had been the largest and most comfortable of Nashoba's buildings. After her sons, William and Kenneth, had entered the Episcopal ministry (by way of the University of the South at Sewanee, sometime around 1890), Sylva lived alone in that place so steeped in mystery and legend, and her very presence kept the romantic character of the property alive. A Memphis newspaper article in 1938 said that "hundreds of Memphians today remember seeing Madame Guthrie, formerly that same Frances Sylva D'Arusmont, and recall the air of mystery which seemed to surround her. Always richly dressed in the continental style of the period, she never appeared in public except in the most formal garb. To a stranger she gave the impression of a woman thoroughly self-contained; courteous, but neither asking nor offering friendship."

William Norman Guthrie, Sylva's oldest son, recalled many years after his mother's death that her disposition "was to react from her mother's [Fanny's] public endeavors. She never spoke of her views until in her old age, although she admired her extravagantly." Of Fanny—whom he of course never knew —William Guthrie spoke bluntly. She was, he said, "cold, austere, courageous, with much unconscious charm, not deigning to exercise any."

Sylva Guthrie died in 1903, and was buried at Elmwood Cemetery in Memphis. The Nashoba land passed to her children, who disposed of it, but the legends surrounding it lived on. (One often repeated tale was that on cold

nights, the mist rising from a sulphur spring took the form of a tall woman and floated across the fields to the spot where Camilla Wright's cabin once stood.) Sylva's obituary in a Memphis newspaper did little to separate fact from fancy in the family history. It said she was not Fanny Wright's daughter but the child of Camilla and "a farmhand of Nashoba . . . an illiterate animal" (presumably Richeson Whitby). The article described Sylva as a "noble, generous, eccentric, weary and worn woman of many romances, devoted to uplifting the poor and despised of the earth"—a description seemingly more suited to Fanny than to either Sylva or Camilla.

During World War I, with anti-German feeling running high in this country, the name of the Germantown community adjacent to the Nashoba site was changed to Nashoba, and then changed back after the war. Today, in a subdivision of modern Early American homes just off U. S. Highway 72 in Shelby County, there is a Neshoba Road on land that once was part of the colony. And nearby, on Riverdale Road, a twenty-five-year-old brick house stands on the foundation timbers that supported the main residence of Nashoba, where Frances Wright and Sylva Guthrie built and nourished their romantic legacy.

Only one vestige of that legacy is still visible: a double row of cedar trees in the side yard of the Riverdale Road home. They once flanked the lane leading to Nashoba, and they were planted by Fanny Wright 150 years ago.

Parallel rows of cedar trees that once flanked the lane leading to Nashoba were planted by Frances Wright 150 years ago, and are the only remaining vestige of the colony. The house beyond them is said to be built upon the foundation timbers of the Nashoba manor house.

3. Rugby:
The "New Jerusalem"
of Thomas Hughes

Wander unaware along State Road 52 into the sylvan stillness of Rugby, Tennessee:

It is a village removed in time from the frenetic hustle of the 1970s, a period piece belonging to Victorian England and to the nineteenth-century settlement of the Cumberland Plateau. The blacktop highway is called Central Avenue, and along the dusty lanes that intersect it—Donnington Road, Farringdon Road, Cumberland Avenue—a dozen or more cottages and manor houses reveal their age in their lines and their origin in their names: Kingstone Lisle, Walton Court, Uffington House. Old England and young America were joined here almost a century ago, and the bond is preserved in the many-gabled roofs, the cupolas, the long verandas, the clapboard siding and gingerbread trim and picket fences.

Near the center of this enchanting and incongruous village are two small but especially imposing structures. One of them, tucked protectively in the hushed shadows of towering pine trees, is a graceful frame church, freshly painted in Victorian shades of rich tan, deep burgundy, and charcoal grey. On the crest of the steeply pitched roof is a bell spire crowned with a wooden cross, and the board-and-batten façade is graced by a circular rose-colored window in the center and single-arched windows on either side of the entrance. Above the glass-paneled door is a sign:

CHRIST CHURCH
EPISCOPAL
RUGBY
Established 1880

The interior of the church is dominated by hand-hewn beams and by an arched double window of stained glass above the altar. Throughout the sanctuary are remembrances of Rugby's past: hanging brass oil lamps, a rosewood organ made in England in 1849, embroidered red and gold altar hangings, and a rich abundance of hand-carved wood, from the pews and bishop's chairs to the pulpit, the communion rail, and the walnut alms basins. Only a handful of Episcopal churches exist on the Cumberland Plateau, and none of them is more steeped in history and tradition than Christ Church.

Across Central Avenue from the church is another small building, a green-shuttered frame structure with a slender cupola on the roof and a fan-shaped window above the front porch. The gold lettering on the glass panes in the double doors is faded but still legible:

HUGHES	OPENED
PUBLIC	Oct. 5th
LIBRARY	1882

Inside, the walls are lined from floor to ceiling with one of the best collections of Victorian literature in the United States—more than 7,000 volumes, most of them contributed by the first residents of the settlement or by English and American publishers at the time the library was opened. Included are many first editions, autographed volumes, and a sizable collection of Victorian-era periodicals from both sides of the Atlantic. From its ornate plaster ceiling to its cane-bottom captain's chairs and heavy walnut reading tables, the library is virtually unchanged from the day its doors first opened. And for most of the twentieth century, it has been the repository for the original records of the Rugby colony—the newspapers, the account books, the letters and diaries and documents that tell of inspiring dreams and rude realities, of births and deaths, successes and failures, beginnings and endings.

How did this embodiment of nineteenth-century British culture penetrate the mountain fastness of East Tennessee? How did there come to be an outpost of the Church of England in this remote place, and a public library worthy of an English city many times the size of Rugby? How have these buildings survived for almost a hundred years? What became of the people who founded this village, and what will become of the heritage they left behind? There are more questions than answers. For all the wealth of records that exist and the scholarly and journalistic accounts that have been written, full understanding of the Rugby past is still elusive, and its future as a living restoration remains to be worked out. But enough is known to fill in most of the blanks, and the remaining uncertainties only add to the fascination of what has been called "the last attempt at English colonization in America."

Rugby was celebrated widely in England and America when it was founded, and much has been written about it since. The essence of the oft-told story is this: Thomas Hughes, a noted English author and social reformer, was

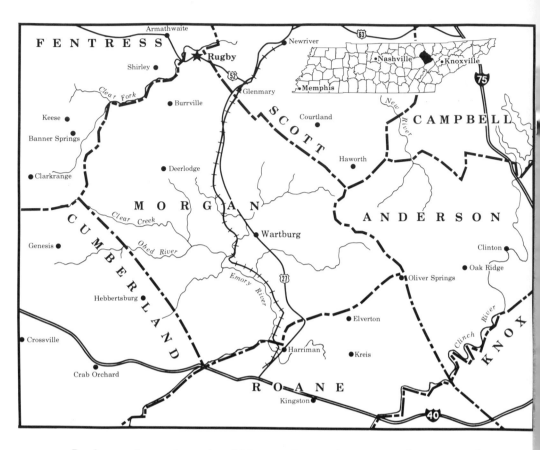

Rugby, at the northern tip of Morgan County, has appeared on maps of Tennessee since the turn of the century. Other nearby communities, including Clarkrange, Deer Lodge, Burrville, and Armathwaite, were also established by participants in the Rugby venture.

the central figure in an Anglo-American venture intended primarily to benefit what Hughes called ''our Will Wimbles''—younger sons of the English upper classes, able and well-educated young men whose talents and energies could find no useful outlets in the anachronistic social structure of the times. The eldest sons got the family inheritance; their younger brothers received, at best, a meager allowance, and to make matters worse, the prevailing social custom held it improper for them to pursue a livelihood in work that was considered beneath them. They could enter law, medicine, the clergy, the press, the public service, but they might lose caste if they turned to the crafts, the trades, and the manual arts—and in any event, there were far more candidates than available positions in those fields.

"So, in sadly increasing numbers," wrote Thomas Hughes, "our Will Wimbles within a year or two of leaving school find themselves stranded. . . . They have tried door after door in vain, and are beginning to find that, for such as they, our time is indeed a cruel one." He was pained to think of what became of the unsuccessful ones, "hanging round and waiting . . . every year less and less fit to fight the battle of life, or do a good stroke of work for themselves, or any one else." England's famed public schools (the same as private schools in America), traditionally the training centers for the nation's intellectual elite, were turning out far more graduates than the learned professions and the other upper-class occupations could absorb, and Hughes asserted that "something like half the number of those who leave our public schools [are] first-rate human material going helplessly to waste . . . drifting on into weary, colourless, middle age."

After a trip to the United States in 1870, Hughes began to dream of establishing a colony there, a place where England's "second sons" could engage in farming and the trades free of the suffocating stigma of caste and class. He subsequently became acquainted with a group of Boston capitalists who held a large tract of land in East Tennessee, and they, together with several wealthy Englishmen, formed the Board of Aid to Land Ownership, Limited, an Anglo-American company with Hughes as president and John Boyle, a London lawyer, as vice president. The Bostonians had acquired the land as a resettlement site for working-class New Englanders idled by an industrial depression, but improved economic conditions diminished interest in the plan. Under Hughes' leadership, the new international company began in 1879 to develop its holdings for what they hoped would be a wave of British immigrants and others ready to create a new community.

The colony was officially opened in October of 1880, and was named Rugby in honor of the famous English school where Hughes had studied and about which he had written in his popular novel, *Tom Brown's School Days*. The Board of Aid to Land Ownership held title to 75,000 acres and options on four or five times as many more, and its first years of activity were favored by widespread and detailed publicity. By the summer of 1881, the colony had 300 residents and more than a dozen buildings either completed or under construction, including the three-story Tabard Inn, named for the famous hostelry in Chaucer's *Canterbury Tales* and containing an original banister from that ancient establishment. It also had a newspaper (*The Rugbeian*), a commissary jointly owned by the shareholding residents, one or two other public buildings, a cafe, a boarding house, several private homes, and a growing reputation as a health resort and a favorite stop-over for traveling dignitaries. And finally, it had a lovely site on a high plain between two deep river gorges, and plenty of land waiting to be cleared for farming and industry.

With those assets and a good beginning, Rugby seemed ready to prove the best hopes of its advocates and to allay the doubts of its detractors, of whom there were more than a few, in England and in the United States. Hughes, the best known and most visible of the organizers, had repeatedly emphasized his hope that Rugby would be a place where manual labor, individual initiative, and community cooperation would produce impressive results. But the high-bred sons of landed gentry seemed improbable practitioners of such enterprise, and skeptics in the press made derisive fun of the tennis courts and bowling greens and bridle paths that somehow got finished before roads and buildings. "Mr. Hughes' purpose was to found a colony of workers," clucked the London *Daily News,* "not to scheme out a pleasure picnic."

The Rugby colonists survived a severe first winter and attacks in the press to greet the spring of 1881 with enough visible signs of progress to keep their optimism high. But serious problems were near at hand: construction fell behind schedule, costs mounted, mistakes in management were made, a hot dry spell set in, and finally, on August 14, an outbreak of typhoid fever claimed the first of seven lives. The Tabard Inn was found to be the source of the contamination, and it was closed. By December, Rugby's population had dropped to sixty, and it was widely reported that the colony was on the brink of collapse.

But Hughes and his English supporters, who by then had taken full control of the Board of Aid to Land Ownership, were determined to make the venture a success. Changes were made in the local leadership and management of the colony, and in the London headquarters as well, where Hughes took great pains to deny rumors that he was about to sever his relationship with the venture. The Tabard, after thorough reconditioning, was reopened; a school-mistress was hired, and classes were begun for the children living in and around Rugby; publishers in the United States and England made generous and heartening contributions to the new library in honor of Hughes. Gradually, the community regained its equilibrium, and by the end of 1882, the population was back up to 150 and growing again. Recovery was slow, running against the continuing tide of economic woes and adverse publicity, but it was steady. Early in 1884 Rugby had between 400 and 450 residents, among them Hastings Hughes, a younger brother of Thomas, and Margaret Hughes, their octogenarian mother. (Thomas himself made regular trips to the

Long before he founded Rugby, Thomas Hughes sat for this portrait (top) by George Frederick Watts; it hangs in the National Gallery in London. Kingstone Lisle, the cottage Hughes had built for himself in the Tennessee community, has been restored (bottom).

colony, but continued to live in England.) The town also had sixty-five buildings either occupied or under construction.

Rugby was at its zenith as a new community. Its residents were engaged in a variety of commercial and vocational ventures that included both private free enterprise and public cooperative ownership. Farming, both individual and collective, was in progress; there was a canning company, and a sawmill, and the commissary; boarding houses, public stables, the cafe, a drug store, blacksmith shops, and a printing office were thriving. The Tabard Inn was the center of the summer holiday traffic, and in 1883 and 1884 the colony had its largest number of vacationing guests.

But its troubles were far from over. The Arnold School, named for Thomas Arnold, Hughes' noted headmaster at Rugby, England, was opened in 1885 and was highly touted as an elite private school in the tradition of the English Rugby, but it was a failure almost from the beginning and never offered the children of the colonists a realistic alternative to public education. The canning factory also failed, and its supply of printed labels for Rugby Brand tomatoes (with the price shown in shillings and pence instead of cents) was never used because not enough tomatoes were raised locally to keep the cannery in operation. The financial backers of the colony continued to lose money, and the residents complained repeatedly about unkept promises and undelivered services. Then, in October of 1884, the Tabard Inn was destroyed in a spectacular fire that consumed all but a few material belongings (one of which was the old banister from the original inn of Chaucer's day).

For three years—until 1887—Rugby managed to hold its own with a reasonably stable population and a precarious but not crumbling financial footing. A new Tabard, more grandiose than its predecessor, was opened in the summer of 1887, and Christ Church was also built that year, allowing the parishioners to vacate their temporary quarters in the public school building. But Arnold School closed, and *The Rugbeian* ceased publication, and shortly after what was to be the last visit to Rugby by Thomas Hughes, his mother died there and his brother moved to Massachusetts. Rugby's heyday was over.

There was no sudden end, but rather a slow and inexorable decline. The Board of Aid to Land Ownership was reorganized in 1892 with a reintroduction of American capital to supplement the British holdings. Thomas Hughes

The original Tabard Inn, named for the "gentil hostelrye" in Chaucer's Canterbury Tales, *was pictured in an early issue of the colony newspaper,* The Rugbeian *(top). In a photograph of unknown origin, eleven people— presumably Rugby colonists—pose in front of the second Tabard Inn (bottom).*

THE RUGBEIAN.

"SHOULDER TO SHOULDER."

VOL. I.   RUGBY, MORGAN CO., TENN., APRIL, 1881.   No. 4.

The Tabard, Rugby.

> —assembled was this compaignye
> In Southwerk at this gentil hostelrye,
> That highte the Tabard——
> *Chaucer's Canterbury Tales.*

Just six months ago when a goodly "compaignye" of Englishmen, some of whom were American citizens, others loyal subjects of Her Gracious Majesty, "assembled at this gentil hostelrye, that highte the Tabard" to lay the foundation stone of Rugby in the New World, there was no need to justify the existence of the building. Its paint and whitewash were barely dry, but without it the ceremony of Oct. the 5th, 1880, could not well have taken place at all. At best the infant settlement would have had to content itself with the maimed rites of a feast of tabernacles. But the hotel had to justify its name; and this also was no difficult matter. It was to be desired that the name of this, the first "hostelrye" opened for public entertainment in a colony whose main object was to bring John and Jonathan closer together, should carry the minds of each back to the days when their forefathers were a truculent, half-amalgamated race, inhabiting a little island off the northwest coast of Europe with no outside interests except those which came from a dislike of quitting their hold of the neighboring continent. This purpose the title in question would have sufficiently answered, but there was another reason which made it still more appropriate, and led to its unanimous adoption by our founders. Some years since a New York gentleman, one of our earliest and truest friends, while on a visit to London strolled across Southwark bridge to "*The Borough*" to find the "Tabard" inn—old, though perhaps with a coat more modern by some hundreds of years than that which it had on when the pilgrims to Canterbury started from its hospitable doors,

and light of the Tabard during the winter of 1880–'81, are likely to keep the first place in their affections for that "gentil hostelrye."

W. H. H.

Public Meeting.

On Saturday evening, April 2d, the largest and most important public meeting that has yet been held in Rugby, assembled in the school-house for the purpose of considering certain hints on sanitary matters that had been submitted to the Board of Aid by Dr. Agnew, of New York. There were present more than one hundred Rugbeians. Mr. John Boyle, Director of the Board, took the Chair, and in explaining the objects of the meeting, said that the townsmen of Rugby were called together

THE TABARD, RUGBY.

This cut, which appeared originally in Harper's Weekly, has been presented by Messrs. Harper Bros., of New York, to The Hughes Public Library.

roads. If the Public Purposes Association were formed it would be the nucleus of great good, but it must be business-like, and have rules. Mr. Boyle then proposed that the Rugby Public Purposes Association be now formed. He invited general discussion, and after saying that the meeting would confer a great favor on him by aiding him to carry out the objects he had in view, called on Mr. W. H. Hughes to second the resolution. Mr. Hughes said that all would recognize the importance of the present meeting. Those who had been here during the past six months had been but a fortuitous concourse of atoms; now, however, there was a head and director among them in the person of Mr. Boyle. The chief matter to be discussed to-night was the sanitary measures to be adopted. During the late trying season it had been difficult to make any great progress, but the time had now come for all true Rugbeians to aid in the good work; he had much pleasure in seconding the resolution. The Chairman having called on others to speak, Mr. Milmow said that he thought we ought to have a church-yard or burial-ground; he hoped that the time was far distant when it would be required, but thought that when the time did come it would be sad to have to bury our children or others dear to us in the nearest field. This suggestion met with expressions of cordial approval. The Chairman then put the resolution formally, and it was carried nem. con. Mr. Blacklock, who was called on to move the next resolution, said that he was glad to be able to begin, "Ladies and Gentlemen"—some ladies having come in since the meeting opened. The resolution put into his hand was: That the first object to which the Association should direct its attention is the sanitary arrangements of the town. (Cheers.) He was glad to hear those cheers. This died in 1896, having lost at least $35,000 of his own money in the venture. A succession of fires, including one that destroyed the second Tabard Inn in 1899, plagued the moribund colony. In the early years of the new century, the corporation's land holdings, by then reduced to about 25,000 acres, were bought by a new group of stockholders, most of them Americans. A number of the original settlers retained their holdings in the area, but most of them left for other parts of the United States or returned to England. Mr. and Mrs. W. T. Walton, both of whom were children of Rugby colonists, remained as caretakers of the church and library until they died in the late 1950s, but Rugby by then was long since a faded and forgotten dream. For seven years—from 1880 to 1887—its residents had, by and large, withstood crisis and catastrophe with chin-up determination and a proper British stiff upper lip. The colony had not only survived—it had even enjoyed brief periods of relative prosperity and success. But from then on, it had slipped steadily toward eventual and inevitable demise.

That, in brief, is the story of the American Rugby, the place Thomas Hughes fondly called his "New Jerusalem." There is broad consensus on the general facts as they have been told and retold in newspapers, magazines, journals, pamphlets and scholarly studies—and as they have been related here. As far as these generalities go, they are supported by the voluminous record of the colony.

But a closer reading of that record and of the various accounts of Rugby raises some intriguing questions, and leaves many of them unanswered. It is doubtful whether the details that are in the record—and those that have been destroyed, or were never recorded—would significantly alter the basic story, but there is certainly sufficient reason to believe that Rugby still offers fertile ground for further inquiry. To support that assertion, it may be useful here to look back again at the story and the record, pausing in a few places to consider small details and to speculate on the missing evidence and unanswered questions.

"We left Cincinnati early in the morning by the Cincinnati Southern Railway," wrote Thomas Hughes in a letter to the *Spectator* in London on September 1, 1880. In that and subsequent letters, he gave a first-person account of the beginning of Rugby, and his accumulated writings on the subject were published in a book the following year. It is a revealing little volume, telling as much about Hughes the man as about his "city of the future."

Thomas Hughes was almost sixty years old at the time Rugby was founded, and he earnestly hoped it would be the culminating achievement of his long career in public life. He was a lawyer, a former member of Parliament, a liberal activist and social reformer, and not least a writer. He had authored half a dozen books before Rugby and was later to complete as many more, but his reputation and his comfortable financial circumstances were a direct result of one volume: *Tom Brown's School Days,* his first book, published in 1857.

The biographies of Hughes describe traits of character and a progression of personal experiences that seem to lead logically to his Tennessee undertaking. He was the second son of a middle-class commoner, a country parish clergyman named John Hughes; and in 1834 he went with his elder brother George to the famous Rugby School to study under Thomas Arnold, an advocate of the then-heretical notion that the country's best schools should not be reserved exclusively for the upper-class sons of noblemen and landed gentry. His eight years at Rugby provided the experiences he was to fictionalize fifteen years later in *Tom Brown's School Days;* they also helped to shape his lifelong interest in education, religion, and democracy.

From Rugby, Hughes went to Oxford, and then to London in 1845 to practice law. There he took an interest in Christian socialism and in its most practical manifestation, the so-called co-operative movement, which had been founded by Robert Owen—the same Robert Owen who had developed the New Harmony community and influenced Frances Wright at Nashoba. Cooperation was an alternative response to highly competitive, laissez-faire free enterprise; it encouraged voluntary public ownership of nonprofit economic enterprises for the benefit of the stockholding members of the collective. Its intent was to elevate the working classes, the common people, and to lessen the inequities of elitism and class privilege, and those objectives closely matched Hughes' own ideals. He was an inclusive man who believed in providing the widest possible latitude and opportunity to all people, and he put his beliefs to work in the co-operative movement, the trade-union movement, the church, the law, and the press. One of his major contributions was to help found, and for ten years to administer, the Working Men's College in London.

Hughes was elected to the House of Commons in 1865, and remained there until 1874, earning a solid reputation as a social reformer and a friend of the working classes. His literary career was already well launched when he entered Parliament, and he used his pen as effectively as his presence to advance the progressive principles he identified himself with. In 1870 he made his first visit to the United States, and in the company of the poet James Russell Lowell he began to shape his dream of a colonization venture that would bring together the several interrelated interests of his life.

It is important to pause here and consider what those interests were and how they converged in his thinking. During the American Civil War, Hughes had been a staunch abolitionist and a Union sympathizer, but in England there had been broad and substantial support for the South. When he was in the United States, his instinctive desire for reconciliation led him to wonder how he might help to heal the remaining wounds, between England and America as well as between the North and the South. Furthermore, he remained deeply committed to the co-operative movement, to trade unions, and to church reform. And finally, he had become concerned with the plight of young Englishmen, upper class and commoners alike, who were leaving the recently reformed public schools in increasing numbers, only to find that lingering caste prejudices and limited economic opportunities left them stranded in idleness. A new community, he began to reason, might offer an excellent opportunity to address all of those concerns at once.

The idea took several years to germinate. Franklin W. Smith, a Boston capitalist whom Hughes had met when he was there, was the leader of a group of men who secured options on 350,000 acres of East Tennessee land in 1878 with the intent of relocating a large number of unemployed New England workers. Cyrus Clarke, the general manager of the land company, moved to the area with about six colonizing families in 1879, but the depression in the East was already improving. Smith, remembering Hughes' interest in colonization, re-established contact with his British friend. Hughes in turn enlisted the support of a wealthy British railway magnate, Henry Kimber, and a prominent London lawyer named John Boyle; and subsequently, the Board of Aid to Land Ownership, Limited, was created.

From the beginning, then, the enterprise that came to be known as Rugby was envisioned as much more than an idealistic utopian retreat for idle English upper-class young men. To Franklin Smith and Cyrus Clarke in Boston, and to Henry Kimber and John Boyle in London, it was primarily a commercial venture, an opportunity to reap financial rewards from the sale of land. The idealism was supplied principally by Thomas Hughes, and he too had more in mind than a bucolic paradise for the wealthy. The land company capitalized on Hughes' prominence; he was its chief spokesman and its drawing card, and what he said about the proposed colony should have discouraged any listeners who expected it to be a pleasure dome.

Hughes described the Will Wimbles he hoped to recruit in the context of the public-school reform movement. They were not, he said, all "boys of gentle birth and bringing up, the sons of the squirearchy"; they included as well the sons of tradesmen and farmers and handicraftsmen, who also were victimized by insufficient opportunity and dog-eat-dog competitiveness. "There is no work for them, of a reasonably hopeful kind, at home," he said, and "caste prejudice against manual labor is too strong.'' Some were not allowed to be farmers and traders and craftsmen, and others could not even if they wished to because land was too costly and wages were too low. What they needed, Hughes asserted, was a chance to begin again, ''across the seas somewhere . . . in a place where what we have been calling the English public-school spirit—the spirit of hardiness, of reticence, of scrupulousness in all money matters, of cordial fellowship, shall be recognized and prevail.''

To the parents and guardians of these young men, Hughes said the colony would be carefully planned in several particulars. There would be a ''central store and mart, open to all,'' owned by the members who bought shares in it, and fully managed by them. There would be one church open to all, ''the property of no single denomination, but of the community.'' Further, Hughes said the company would provide living quarters and meals at a cheap rate, ''and [we] have arranged that all the work on our unsold lands—in gardening, planting, clearing, cultivating—shall be done by such settlers as care to undertake it, by piece work, paid for by us at the rate current in the neighbour-hood.'' And when the settlers were ready to buy land for themselves, he added, it would be available at a good price.

''And there we leave him,'' Hughes concluded. ''If with these helps he cannot fall in with the life about him, keep himself well by his own work, and make himself an acceptable member of the new society, he is not the sort of person required for this experiment.''

Thomas Hughes was an outspoken opponent of government socialism, and of communism. He made a careful distinction between state socialism and Christian socialism, advocating the voluntary individual cooperation of the latter as an equitable and rational alternative to the former. He believed in hard work, in manual labor, in mutual and uncoerced fellowship, in religious tolerance, in temperance. And those were the principles upon which he wanted the new colony to be founded. If the other leading figures in the development shared those views with equal conviction, the record does not show it clearly.

''We left Cincinnati early in the morning,'' Hughes began. He was on his way to the formal opening of the colony, full of great expectations, and keeping a notebook of his observations for his own use and the benefit of his readers in the *Spectator*. The railroad had been opened from Cincinnati to Chattanooga for less than six months, but its passenger cars were filled to capacity, and Hughes noted with surprise ''the apparently excellent terms on which the white and coloured people were consorting, even in the Kuklux regions through which we came.'' It was, he had been told, ''the most lawless [region] in the United States," yet he observed "the familiar and apparently friendly footing on which the races met," and added that he found the blacks to be "such friendly folk, that I regret their absence from this same Alpine settlement."

The last fifty miles to the station—named Sedgemoor by the earliest arriving settlers—was through dense forests. When the train arrived at five o'clock in the afternoon, Hughes was greeted "by four or five young Englishmen . . . every one of whom was well known to me in ordinary life, but whom for the first moment I did not recognize. I had seen them last clothed in frock-coat and stove-pipe hat. . . . [Now they wore] Broad-brimmed straw or felt hats, the latter very battered and worse for wear; dark blue jerseys, or flannel shirts of varying hue; breeches and gaiters, or long boots."

Several saddle-horses, a light buggy, and a mule wagon for luggage were in wait for eleven men going the last seven miles to the colony, and Hughes was eager "to get through the intervening miles of forest tracks in time for tea up here." They arrived at dusk, and saw "the bright gleam of light under the verandahs of two sightly wooden houses," and on closer inspection found several other buildings—including the inn—under construction, an unnoted number of settlers and construction workers present, and "two young ladies, who had hurried down before us to visit their brother, a settler on the plateau."

In his month's wait for the October 5 dedication of the colony, Hughes became familiar with his surroundings. He praised the food ("tea and fresh water for drink, plates of beef or mutton, apple sauce, rice, tomatoes, peach pies or puddings, and several kinds of bread"). He was informed that someone would black his boots at night, as if he were in a proper English hostelry, and he was "at first inclined to protest . . . that we should be followed by the lumber of civilisation so closely! Will boots be blacked, I wonder, in the New Jerusalem?" He was charmed by the colony's "forester" (gardener and groundskeeper), a fifty-nine-year-old man named Amos Hill who had been born near Rugby, England, and had lived for thirty years in the United States, the last thirteen of them on the Cumberland Plateau. Hughes found the hotel nearly completed and already named the Tabard, with its prized stair railing from the old English inn to be marked with an inscribed brass plate. He noted that "the drink question has reared its baleful head here" because "two young natives 'toted over' some barrels of whisky," after which there was "no peace for the manager." The effect was sudden: "On Saturday last the crisis came, and some twenty men got drunk and gambled all through Sunday, getting very near a free fight in the end; and on Monday half the work collapsed." It would not do, Hughes concluded. State law prohibited the sale of liquor within four miles of a rural school. "The feeling of the community is vigorously temperate," Hughes noted, and went on to say that "if we are to have influence with the poor whites and blacks, we must be above suspicion ourselves. So no liquor will be procurable at the Tabard, and those who need it will have to import it for themselves." (One who apparently needed it was Hughes' brother, Hastings, who had preceded him there and who remained as a leading resident for about eight years. He was competent and well liked, but on more than one occasion he was criticized for public drunkenness.)

Hughes described for his readers in England the three miles of cleared paths through the woods, leading from the buildings to the banks of the Clear Fork and White Oak rivers, deep in the gorges. And he told of being hailed by "one of the boys . . . in flannels, with racquet in hand, on his way to the lawn-tennis ground." He witnessed the opening match there—two sets of doubles involving three young men and a woman—and noted that "The Rugby Tennis Club consists to-day of seven members, five English and two native." Almost as an afterthought, he added that the name Rugby "was adopted unanimously on our return in twilight from the tennis-ground." The land company had been calling the settlement Plateau; Hughes found the name uninspiring, and with his young companions he deemed it changed to Rugby—and got no argument about it.

Judiciously tucked between the lines of his correspondence, there is a faint hint of disquiet in the words of Thomas Hughes. Here were people at work converting his fond dream to reality—but here too were bootblacks and "Lover's Walks," tennis courts and bootleg whisky. "The thought occurs," he wrote: "are our swans—our visions, already so bright, of splendid crops, and simple life, to be raised and lived in this fairyland—to prove geese? I hope not. It would be the downfall of the last castle in Spain I am ever likely to build."

On opening day, Hughes addressed the assembled residents and guests on the veranda of the inn, which the previous night had been occupied for the first time, accommodating seventy or eighty guests, including the Episcopal bishop of Tennessee, the mayor of Chattanooga, and dignitaries from Knoxville, Cincinnati, and Boston. It was a memorable day, he later wrote: "The glorious southern sun had fairly vanquished rain and mist, and the whole plateau was ablaze with the autumn tints. . . . Rugby outdid herself . . . in a way which astonished even her oldest and most enthusiastic citizens." In his remarks to the audience, Hughes stated in some detail his own hopes and aspirations for the colony, and the philosophical basis for them.

At the outset, he sought to dispel "an impression which seems to have got abroad" that Rugby was intended to be an exclusively English colony. "Our settlement is open to all who like our principles and our ways," he said; "Englishmen and Americans can stand shoulder to shoulder, and work with one mind and one heart for the same great end."

Hughes then addressed himself to "our starting point . . . the idea which we are to try to realize." He professed to have "no sympathy whatever with the state communism of Europe, represented by Karl Marx," and "no vision whatever to realize of a paternal state, the owner of all property, reserving all profits for the community, and paying no dividends to individuals." The laws relating to private property and family life, he said, would either suffice for the community or be modified "in certain directions as our corporate conscience ripens." But he recognized and emphasized the need "to establish a *community* . . . to have *something* in common . . . *some* bond which binds us all together." What the common bond should be he described in these words:

> Well, in the first place, there is this lovely corner of God's earth which has been intrusted to us. What, as a community, is our first duty with regard to it? It is, to treat it lovingly and reverently. We can add little, perhaps, to its natural beauty, but at least we can be careful to spoil it as little as possible.
>
> First as to the laying out of our town here. There shall be ample provision for all public wants from the first. We have two beautiful streams which will be a delight for ever to those who dwell here, if they are left free for the use and enjoyment of all. In laying out the town we have reserved a strip of various widths along the banks, which will remain common property, kept in order by the municipal authorities. Then there must be reservations for parks, gardens, and recreation grounds. With this example and ideal before their eyes, we may hope that the lots which pass into the hands of private owners will also be handled with an eye to the common good.

From the emphasis on preservation and enjoyment of the area's natural beauty, Hughes moved next to a discussion of the colony's buildings, which he said would be devoid of "superfluous decoration" and "simple and even rough in materials and construction." The first public buildings "will consist . . . of a church and school house, and then of a court-house and town-hall." As for the private structures, "every man will build his house according to his own fancy, and use it for whatever purpose he pleases, except for the sale of intoxicating liquors, which will be strictly prohibited."

Hughes noted that "the survival of the fittest is recognized as a natural law, which means that men will always live upon, and not for, one another." Such a philosophy was clearly repugnant to him; he said it should be modified by reason and agreement, rather than accepted unconditionally. To that end, he described further the combination of public and private enterprise he wanted Rugby to develop:

We have all of us a number of imperative wants which must be provided for and satisfied day by day. We want food, clothes, furniture, and a great variety of things besides, which our nurture and culture have made all but essential to us. These must all be provided here, either by each of us for himself, or by some common machinery. Well, we believe that it can be done best by a common machinery. We have a ''commissary'' already established, a public institution. Our wish is to make this commissary a centre of supply, and that every settler, every householder here, shall become a member and part owner of it, with small shares of five dollars each. In this way we shall have a common interest and common property, and in the supplying of our own daily wants shall feel that if one member suffers, all suffer. In this way we may be rid once for all of the evils which have turned retail trade into a keen and anxious and, generally, a dishonest scramble in older communities: rid of adulteration, of false pretenses, of indebtedness, of bankruptcy.

Hughes said that the Board of Aid to Land Ownership would use large tracts of property around the town site for pasturing livestock, and that too would be a public undertaking in which the colonists could buy shares. But he warned that anyone who might be attracted to Rugby by a desire to make a quick profit, either from the land or from public or private enterprise, was not the sort of settler the colony needed or wanted. ''Speaking for myself,'' he said, ''I look with distrust rather than with hope on very rapid pecuniary returns. So far as I have been able to judge, these new settlements are being, as a rule, dwarfed and demoralised by hurrying forward in the pursuit of gain. Then follows that feverish activity of mercantile speculation which is the great danger and, to my mind, the great disgrace of our time.''

On the subject of individual freedom, Hughes was forthright; there should be no attempt to interfere with any person's private behavior, or to restrict personal liberty. ''Every one will be free to worship in his own way,'' he said, ''and to provide for whatever religious ministrations he requires, out of his own funds and according to his own ideas.'' To assure that freedom, he advocated the construction of a single church building that could be used by ''the members of different Christian denominations'' for ''their several acts of worship.''

Finally, Hughes concluded with this statement of philosophical purpose for his new community:

Our aim and hope are to plant on these highlands a community of gentlemen and ladies; not that artificial class which goes by those grand names, both in Europe and here, the joint product of feudalism and wealth, but a society in which the humblest members, who live by the labour of their own hands, will be of such strain and culture that they will be able to meet princes in the gate, should any such strange persons ever present themselves before the gate tower of Rugby in the New World.

With the benefit of more than ninety years of hindsight, it is easy to raise valid questions about Rugby from Hughes' speech—from what he said, what he implied, and what he made no allusion to at all. He spoke in detail of having a combination of public and private ownership, but said nothing at all about governance of the colony—and in fact, throughout the Rugby record, there is virtually no mention of elections or officeholders. In reality, Rugby was a company town, a benevolent oligarchy in which Hughes and a few others made all of the major decisions—and if the settlers longed for a more democratic community, they kept their longings to themselves. The "municipal authorities" Hughes referred to were not rank-and-file Rugbeians; they were the unelected hierarchy. That fact helps to explain why the chronicle of Rugby is dominated by a handful of prominent names, while the hundreds of residents—the "plain folk"—seem in contrast to be faceless and anonymous. To be sure, there were many interesting and colorful people at Rugby in addition to its leaders, but in the paternalistic scheme of things, they were never very visible.

Hughes, in his address, was eloquent in his advocacy of religious freedom and cooperation, and his words of warning about preserving the environment and protecting the consumer from unfair and unrestrained commercialism have a contemporary ring when they are read now. His assertion that profit-seeking was not a valid motive for colonizing could well be taken to heart by the builders of many twentieth-century new communities. Even so, one is left with a mental image of the real, rude Rugby as a far cry from the Rugby of Hughes' dreams. The cooperative raising of livestock which he said the company would establish as a public industry "at once" never was started at all, nor was there ever a courthouse. He talked of hard work and sacrifice almost in the same breath with raising a community of refined ladies and gentlemen, and saw no inconsistency in it, but the two proved a hard mixture to brew. He envisioned Britishers and Americans, Yankees and Southerners, noblemen and commoners, whites and blacks, men and women, refined schoolboys and rough mountaineers engaged in a shoulder-to-shoulder striving for the common good, but the combination of people he got was all too human. Hughes was the one who conjured up the dream, gave it life and

Christ Church, Episcopal, has been in continuous use at Rugby since it was built in 1887, and looks much the same today (top) as it did then. So does the Hughes Public Library, shown here (below) in a photograph taken soon after it was opened in 1882.

voice, christened it and praised it and wished it Godspeed. But then he returned to England, and the formidable task of day-by-day development was left in other hands.

After he was back in London, Hughes received a letter from a young colonist telling him that as of the twenty-ninth of October—just three weeks after the formal opening—Rugby had a population of about 120, but "no great assemblage of public schoolmen here at present—one each of Rugby, Wellington, Malvern, and Brighton, will about fill the bill." By January, when the population had passed 200, the first issue of *The Rugbeian* noted that 20 percent of the residents were natives of the mountains, and another 40 percent were Americans from other parts of the country, north and south; only 40 percent were British, and that presumably included not just young "second sons" but also a number of adults, including Hastings Hughes and John Boyle, the London barrister. And there was also an undetermined number of women, English and American. In sum, the description of Rugby as a colony of highbred, upper-class young Englishmen is incomplete, if not inaccurate. From the beginning, it was a mixture of many people from many places. It had a physician from Boston, a civil engineer from Cincinnati, a librarian from Germany, one family of blacks, and many families of whites from Tennessee. One partial list of colonists during the years from 1879 to 1885 includes 226 names, of whom at least 100 were females, and a later list, also incomplete, totals 313 people, about half of them women. There is no complete list of Rugby colonists in existence, but about 100 different surnames can be identified. Some were families of ten or more people, others were single men or single women, and several, with names like Bertz and Molyneux and Onderdonk, were not British. Rugby may never have had a majority-British population, and almost certainly never had a majority of younger sons of the English gentry—even though they have been commonly depicted as its principal residents.

Perhaps that is because Hughes addressed his appeal primarily to them. Back in England at the end of 1880, he wrote magazine articles and made speeches in the public schools (including Rugby) urging young men to go west—if they were "prepared for some years, during the working hours of the day, to live the life of a peasant." There was work to be done at Rugby, he said—farming, lumbering, carpentry, masonry—and after hours, "a cultivated society, within easy reach of all." He told them to take only the barest essentials (mainly "two or three stout suits of clothes"), and a little money. Passage from London to Rugby by steamer and railroad could be had for as little as $42.50, third class ($105 first class). Those with previous training and experience who could support themselves with a job when they arrived would need little more; others not ready to take a regular job could get room and board for a year for $300 while they prepared themselves for self-sufficiency. Hughes invited his audiences to ''help in drawing as close as possible the bonds which unite [England] to the United States. . . . What we English want, looking to the future, is, not only that England and America should be fast friends, but that the feeling of union in the States themselves should be developed as soundly and rapidly as possible.''

To his credit, Hughes never consciously attempted to mislead anyone about Rugby. He avoided making overblown promises, and he consistently gave fair warning of the difficulties to be faced. He spoke the truth as he saw it. But he was not a particularly practical man, not a realist but an idealist at heart, and he had a tendency to expect the highest motives and the noblest acts of almost everyone. To a fault, he was uncritical of his fellow man: sympathetic, forgiving, accepting. And his fellow man, all too often, turned out to be less exalted than Hughes assumed. While he was busy extolling the virtues of international brotherhood and voluntary economic cooperation in a cultured community of gentlemen agrarians, the principal figures in the building of Rugby were beginning to find out how different their motives and ideals and expectations were. Ultimately, the differences proved to be irreconcilable.

One of the first and most divisive difficulties the colony faced concerned leadership. Franklin Smith, the largest American financier of the land company, pulled out early, but Cyrus Clarke, his chief agent, became an investor and a resident in the area, and a man to be reckoned with in the decision-making process. Henry Kimber, the principal British investor, made frequent trips to Rugby and maintained a long-term interest in it, but John Boyle was his resident representative, and as vice president of the company, he too exerted a strong influence. In addition, there was Hastings Hughes, who held his brother's power of attorney—and by virtue of it, a major voice in the determination of policy. Clarke had made the initial land purchases; Boyle had picked the site for the town; Hastings Hughes was his brother's stand-in. The three men were in contention for primacy, and they did not get along with one another personally. Clarke was strong-willed and assertive, and widely regarded as an opportunist and a land shark. Boyle was an arrogant man whom the settlers derisively called ''Lord God Almighty Boyle.'' The two men shared a desire to make Rugby a financial success, but on virtually everything else they were at odds, and their enmity eventually resulted in a fist fight. The Hughes brothers took sides in neither camp, being less interested in economic squabbles than in the philosophical and cultural aspects of the colony.

In spite of these internal difficulties and a bitterly cold first winter, the settlers celebrated a cheerful Christmas with homemade plum pudding and welcomed 1881 with dogged good humor. The rivers froze over, and ice and mud made the dirt roads at times almost impassable, but construction managed somehow to go slowly forward, and the population continued to increase. Christ Church was organized, as was a library club and other social and recreational groups, and the new three-story school building, completed in advance of the organization of a school, served as a church and meeting place for a variety of community activities. The commissary did a thriving business, the newspaper was launched, and the Tabard Inn was attracting a growing number of visitors, among them the widowed daughter of Charles A. Dana, editor of the New York *Sun*. Publicity, both in praise and in criticism of the Rugby experiment, filled the press on both sides of the Atlantic, and the net effect of it was favorable to the colony's early growth, proving the old adage that any mention, even critical, is better than no mention at all. Whatever it was, Rugby was not ignored.

Some farming was begun. A Scottish wool grower started a 400-acre sheep farm three miles from the town, and land was cleared for at least four other agricultural ventures, ranging in size from 41 to 387 acres. A score or more settlers bought lots for private residences. *The Rugbeian* reacted strongly against criticism in the English and American press, saying it was uninformed and untrue, and should be ignored. Margaret Hughes, the eighty-three-year-old mother of Thomas and Hastings, arrived in May 1881 after a highly publicized journey and took up residence there, to the delight of the settlers, most of whom apparently venerated their "founding father" and greatly admired his resident younger brother.

But serious troubles were near at hand. Legal difficulties were encountered in obtaining clear titles to much of the land. British and American investors quarreled among themselves over advertising and publicity, and most of all over mounting expenses and spending priorities. And among the colonists, there was growing dissatisfaction with the leadership of Clarke and Boyle and the failure of the company to deliver the programs and services they had promised would be forthcoming. Sanitary conditions were often discussed, notably at a large public meeting in April 1881. The colony was still depending upon springs and one well for its fresh water, and though the dry summer season was approaching, the promised public water works had not been built. "Health was not a matter of chance or accident," the newspaper quoted a speaker at the public meeting as saying. "It had laws, silent and constant; if they were violated the penalty must come."

The residents had been led to expect a school as well, but in May, when a census showed fifty-six children in the community, no school had been organized. No satisfactory method of waste and garbage disposal had been devised. Land prices had been raised—in some instances, from $2 to $20 an acre. There were complaints of noise and rowdiness at night around the inn and the boarding houses, and some people charged that whisky was easily obtainable on certain evenings simply by "giving a few shrill whistles." There were assertions that the land was poor and unfit for farming and that the settlers had been shamefully deceived. They had not come expecting "all beer and skittles," they said; Rugby was not Utopia, and was not intended to be—but not everyone was carrying his fair share of the load, and the land company was reneging on its promises. It was time for greater sacrifice and a larger investment, and time too, perhaps, for a change in management. Rumors spread that Thomas Hughes was planning to abandon the colony, that it was near collapse, that it would be relocated in Minnesota.

Then, on August 14, the worst began to happen: Osmond Dakeyne, a co-editor of *The Rugbeian,* died of "typhoid symtoms." Within six weeks, seven young people died of the disease, and more than twenty cases were reported. The contamination was traced to the Tabard Inn. Its well was sealed off, and then the hotel itself was shut down. There were cries of outrage in the press, charges and countercharges were thrown about, and settlers left in droves. By the end of December 1881, the population had dropped from 300 to 60, and financial disaster was imminent. A representative of the Board of Aid to Land Ownership in London wrote to John Boyle: "I have expended weeks in trying to get the shareholders together, but they exhibit a perfect apathy in the matter. . . . I have to inform you that locally, you must now fight the battle yourself. You must put down every expense and carry on nothing that does not show a profit on the books of the Company; and further expenditures will be at your own risk." *The Rugbeian* said solemnly that in the eyes of the company, "the Rugby Colony is a failure," and it added the belief of the editors that "Thomas Hughes does not know, and has not known all along, the true position, at any time, of the Rugby Colony."

Back in London, the news was a crushing blow to Hughes. He had problems enough without Rugby. He had lost much of his wealth (by some accounts, as much as $250,000) and no small part of his reputation, at least indirectly as a result of the colony, and the social movements he had so staunchly supported—the co-operatives and the trade unions—had begun to move in directions he was unwilling to go. Furthermore, his wife had no interest in Rugby, and she and their children refused to go there. Hughes himself did not return to the colony until the fall of 1883, and his absence was undoubtedly a crucial factor in its continuous tribulations.

But Hughes had no intention of giving up on his New Jerusalem. Against the wishes of his family, the barbs of his political enemies, and the criticism of the press, he asserted his influence in person with the British financiers of the company and in correspondence with his brother and the other leaders of the settlement in Tennessee. The result was a change in management. Robert Walton, an Irishman from Cincinnati and one of the original settlers at Rugby, was made general manager. A civil engineer, he had come at first to design and lay out the town, and had stayed to become one of its most popular and respected residents. Under his leadership, the community began a concerted effort to recoup its losses.

New settlers began trickling in, and by the beginning of 1883 the population had risen to 150. The Tabard was operating again, and for the first time it had competent management in the person of Abner Ross, who had come from the Palmer House in Chicago. Summer tourist trade picked up, the library was opened, school was at last in session, the public water works was in operation, and efforts were made to open the canning factory and other industries. By early 1884, Rugby was larger than ever—it had some 450 residents and 65 buildings—and in spite of the fire that destroyed the Tabard, the community managed for about three years to have some stability and an acceptable minimum of conflict.

But the odds against its continued growth and survival remained high. The United States was in the midst of a long-wave depression marked by strikes and boycotts, declining wages and prices, and numerous bankruptcies. A period of farm prosperity had been followed by a decline in commodity prices and, in 1887, a long drought. Rugby could not escape the effects of all that. Its industries did not pan out, and its agricultural ventures were not particularly successful either. Land prices fell again, and the company, which had sold seventy-four parcels of property in its first two years of operation (until the typhoid epidemic), could sell only thirty-two parcels in the next four years, and the trend continued downward. Nationally, the taint of communism was in the air, and the anxious and somewhat defensive settlers at Rugby responded by selling their commissary to a private entrepreneur. The Board of Aid to Land Ownership, with Henry Kimber remaining as its principal investor, still could not resist the temptation to try to rule the colony from London, and Robert Walton, its $125-a-month resident manager, was frequently hindered by the board's interference. Through it all—and in spite of Thomas Hughes' clear statement of principles and objectives—there remained a fundamental confusion about precisely what Rugby was intended to be. The motives of idealism and philanthropy and profit-making were constantly in conflict; and while some people sought to make it a farming community or a trading center, others wanted it to be a health resort or a tourist haven, and still others envisioned it as a utopia for young Englishmen or a leisurely retreat for the upper class.

Finally, the young Englishmen, who were the most visible if not the most numerous segment of the Rugby populace, proved to be on the whole ill-suited for the rigors of community-building in the wilderness. To be sure, some of them possessed the virtues of thrift and industriousness that Thomas Hughes praised so highly, and they performed admirably and with notable success. But many were not so constituted; they were naïve and uninitiated idealists and adventurers, grumblers, loafers, snobs, gilded playboy pioneers with too much money from home and too little understanding of their surroundings to be anything more than a hindrance to their fellow colonists and an irritation to the mountain people whose native land they had entered. From all indications, the misfits were not a majority of the young Englishmen who came to the colony, and as we have seen, the young Englishmen as a group probably constituted a minority of the total community. But in most of the assessments of Rugby's failure, the lion's share of blame has been laid on the soft-handed sons of gentry, who were "long on pretty plans and short on elbow grease and common sense," and "mixing tea and tennis and leisurely pursuits in the land of the long rifle and the coonskin cap."

In retrospect, that criticism seems unduly harsh. If anyone could have been held primarily responsible for the collapse of the colony, it was not the young men—or even Thomas Hughes, the founding father—but the English and American investors who ran the Board of Aid to Land Ownership. They seemed never to have understood or supported what Hughes hoped to accomplish, and in the end they were done in by the very same mindless pursuit of profit that Hughes from the beginning had called "the great disgrace of our time."

But perhaps that too is an excessively severe judgment. Many things contributed to the decline, not least of them being fire and drought and disease. It might have been that better planning or better management or better luck would have produced a different result—but it might also have been that such circumstances would only have delayed the inevitable. In any event, 1887 turned out to be the beginning of the end for Rugby. Christ Church was completed in that year, and so was the new Tabard Inn, but the Arnold School was already being written off as a failure, and *The Rugbeian* ceased publication, the library was deep in debt, and settlers began to leave. Thomas Hughes was there in the fall for his fifth consecutive annual visit, but shortly after he left—on October 5, the seventh anniversary of the colony—his mother died, and the rector of Christ Church said with prophetic accuracy in his eulogy of her that "the great binding link between Rugby and the family of Mr. Thomas Hughes has been removed." Hughes was never to return. When his brother Hastings departed for New England, it was in truth the end of the Hughes connection.

When Thomas Hughes died in 1896 at the age of seventy-four, his obituaries scarcely mentioned Rugby, apparently considering it an embarrassing aberration in an otherwise admirable and productive life. Hughes would have been deeply hurt by that; he went to his grave treasuring his memory of the colony as "amongst the evergreen spots of my life." In 1892, when he was past seventy and Rugby was past saving, he conveyed his unquenchable faith and optimism in a letter to his friend Charles Kemp, the Rugby physician. "I can't help feeling and believing," he wrote, "that good seed was sown when Rugby was founded and that someday the reapers . . . will come along with joy, bearing heavy sheaves with them. Whether I shall live to see it may be doubtful. . . . However, whether I can ever come again or not, you, my dear friend, will always know how truly I'm with you in the famous fight you are making to plant a righteous and prosperous colony in those fascinating mountains."

The Board of Aid was reorganized in 1892 under a new name, and Robert Walton stayed on as general manager until his death in 1907. Henry Kimber kept his interest in the land until his death, and his heirs were involved in still another company reorganization in 1909, when it became the Rugby Land Company, with Americans controlling most of the stock. By then, the second Tabard had been destroyed by fire, the school building had also burned, and Rugby was long since finished as a vibrant community. Walton's son, W. T. Walton, and his wife, who previously had been married to a son of Henry Kimber, managed the public buildings there from 1907 until they died in the late 1950s. The remaining homes were privately owned, a few of them by descendants of the early colonists, and the rest of the land—all that remained of the more than 400,000 acres of holdings and options—was divided and sold.

One final dimension of the Rugby experiment needs to be put in place. While the little village and its contingent of young upper-class Englishmen were the primary—often the exclusive—objects of public attention, Rugby was not the only town to emerge within the territory held by the Board of Aid. There are, even now, several communities that originated, directly or indirectly, as a result of Rugby. Sedgemoor, the railroad station that later was called Rugby Road (and still has a station sign bearing that name), is now the village of Elgin. Clarkrange is named for Cyrus Clarke. Burrville, Skene, Glades, Deer Lodge, and Armathwaite were established by people who were affiliated in one way or another with Rugby. Another community, Coal Hill, once had an Episcopal church with about a hundred communicants, and the population of the village was made up almost entirely of Welsh coal miners and their families who came to Tennessee because of Rugby. When the entire holdings of the Board of Aid are taken into consideration, it becomes clear that far more than the village of Rugby itself was being developed. And ironically, that perspective strengthens the image of Thomas Hughes. His critics called him a hopeless romantic and a naïve idealist, but he repeatedly and consistently advocated a merging of diverse cultures into a cooperative and industrious new community. He had an appreciation for the native mountain people of the Cumberland Plateau and for the working classes of England and America, and he believed they and his Will Wimbles could work compatibly toward a society unencumbered by the strictures of caste and class. But too many of those who allied themselves with his dream simply wanted to transplant the good life from England, or from Boston. In the words of one disillusioned colonist, they created not a cooperative multicultural society but an "Old World and conservative colony," antagonistic not only to the native mountaineers but to others—including the Welsh coal miners—who came looking for work and opportunity rather than quick fortunes and a life of leisure.

So Rugby failed. In the correspondence of W. T. Walton, there is a letter he wrote in 1926 that describes the lonely aftermath of what he called "a unique and impractical colonization scheme." Twilight, he said, "descended upon Rugby in a very short time, and deepened into the shades of night. . . . At Rugby, there is, and has long been, a depressing quiet, unbroken save for the songs of the birds in the towering trees which, as of yore, adorn what were once winding avenues through the forest."

Midway through the 1970s, more than a thousand acres of land and the remaining original buildings at Rugby were in the hands of about fifty people who formed the backbone of the Rugby Restoration Association, a young organization intent on breathing new life into the old settlement. The association was formed in 1966 by a small group of interested Tennesseans, and it now owns the school building (a replacement of the original structure), Kingstone Lisle (a cottage built for Thomas Hughes in 1884), the office building of the Board of Aid to Land Ownership, a few other buildings, and several lots where original structures once stood. A separate but related board owns the library, and Christ Church belongs to the Episcopal Diocese of Tennessee, and those groups have an active interest in the restoration of the community.

The library and the church remain today, as they were in the 1880s, the focal point of Rugby. They have survived not just as physical reminders of the past but as living symbols of the Victorian period, of the spirit of Rugby, and of Thomas Hughes' devotion to the life of the mind and the soul. The library has been called "a Rip Van Winkle of books," and indeed, its contents and appearance are virtually unchanged from the October day in 1882 when the building was opened to the public. Under its original charter, the library has been governed continuously by a single, self-perpetuating board whose members are elected for life. Christ Church, quintessentially English in its architecture as well as its theological traditions, has been in continuous use since it was completed in the fall of 1887, and some of its furnishings, including the altar and the organ, were brought to Rugby the year the colony opened.

The Rugby Restoration Association's first director, Brian Stagg, was a seventeen-year-old resident of nearby Deer Lodge and a freshman at the University of the South at Sewanee when he was chosen to lead the organization in 1966. In 1973, he wrote *A Distant Eden*, a brief history of the colony and a guide to its remaining original buildings—of which one, Roslyn, became his home. Before his untimely death in 1976, Stagg worked with his companions in the association to achieve what he called "a positive, active restoration, rather than a stand-still preservation or a museum." They succeeded in having Rugby listed in the National Register of Historic Places, and received help in their various undertakings not only from the overseers of the library and church but also from the Tennessee Historical Commission, the University of Tennessee, the Tennessee Department of Conservation, the Tennessee Valley Authority, the East Tennessee Development District, the U.S. Department of the Interior, and numerous other public and private organizations and individuals.

In 1974, Congress designated a 120,000-acre section of the Cumberland Plateau in Tennessee and Kentucky as the Big South Fork National River and Recreation Area, and directed that the region of forests and river gorges be preserved in its wilderness state and protected from commercial development. The boundary of the new federal area follows the Clear Fork River and the White Oak Creek, which surround Rugby on three sides. The fourth side, south of the village, is in the hands of private owners who have made a pledge to donate 100 acres of it to the restoration association as a protective green belt. The Tennessee General Assembly has passed the Rugby Historic Preservation Act in a further attempt to assure the perpetuation of the village, and it was announced in 1975 that one consequence of the federal river and recreation area project will be the construction of a third Tabard Inn. Thus, Rugby may yet survive as an active embodiment of the spirit that led to its creation almost 100 years ago.

No doubt Thomas Hughes would be pleased. The combination of public and private initiative by natives and newcomers, young and old, to make Rugby a vibrant and productive community seems very close to what he had in mind when he first dreamed of creating a "prosperous colony in these fascinating mountains."

A library was one of the first structures Thomas Hughes wanted built at Rugby. It was opened two years after the colony was founded, as the faded lettering on its arched double doors indicates. The library contains a valuable collection of Victorian literature.

4. Ruskin: Julius Wayland and "The Co-operative Commonwealth"

There is no explaining the strange career of Julius Augustus Wayland. Born poor in Vincennes, Indiana, in 1854, he went on to become (in chronological order) a successful printer and a Republican capitalist in his home state, a postmaster and an alleged carpetbagger in post–Civil-War Missouri, a prosperous real estate speculator in Colorado, a Socialist newspaper publisher back home in Indiana, the founder of a utopian Socialist colony in Tennessee, and the publisher of a Kansas-based newspaper with a national following of left-wing political reformers. He has been called "a Victorian Tom Paine" and "the greatest propagandist of Socialism that has ever lived." His Kansas paper, *Appeal to Reason,* attained a circulation of more than 150,000. He introduced Eugene V. Debs to Socialism, and Debs went on to run for President of the United States five times and to become the most famous Socialist in American history (with the possible exception of Norman Thomas). Wayland suggested to Upton Sinclair the idea of writing a book exposing deplorable conditions in the Chicago stockyards, and Sinclair subsequently turned it into his muckraking classic, *The Jungle.* As a convert to Socialism, Wayland attacked monopolies and free enterprise with unflagging zeal, but he never lost the knack for turning a profit; and although he gave most of what he made to his adopted cause, he did not die a poor man. He did, however, die tragically. In 1912, after his party had lost another election and his paper had lost its broad appeal, the man who had optimistically expected "the coming nation" to be a Socialist state finally gave up in despair and took his own life. And then, the strangest thing of all about Julius Wayland: his visibility and influence and notoriety evaporated almost instantly; he seemed to disappear without a trace; he was quickly forgotten, and has hardly been remembered since. The longest account of his life yet written apparently is a twenty-two-page article by Howard Quint in a 1949 issue of the *Mississippi Valley Historical Review.* Not even the most comprehensive of American biographical reference books gives so much as the vital statistics of the man who made Socialism understandable and acceptable to tens of thousands of Americans.

The biographers have overlooked a fascinating character. Wayland is worth remembering for his skill as a propagandist, his political and social influence, and his colorful excursion from Republicanism to Socialism. And perhaps most of all, he should be remembered as the founder of Ruskin, a Middle Tennessee utopian colony that attracted settlers from all over the United States before it fell victim to its own internal flaws and to the American legal system it so critically disdained.

The last decade of the nineteenth century was a period of great political and economic instability in the United States. Grover Cleveland was elected President in 1892, the only man ever to win that office, lose it, and then win it again. Populism was on the rise, and William Jennings Bryan, as the standard-bearer for the Democrats and the Populists, made a strong bid for the presidency in 1896. The stock market crashed in the Panic of 1893, and Jacob Coxey led his "army" of the unemployed in a march on Washington. The opulence of the "money barons"—the Carnegies, Morgans, Rockefellers and others—stood in vivid contrast to the poverty of the masses; and men who called themselves Populists or Socialists or Communists advocated numerous alternatives to the inequitable system of unrestrained private enterprise. It was also a busy time for experimental utopian communities: by one estimate, more than eighty such colonies were scattered across the United States at the close of the century.

On the eve of the Panic of 1893, Julius Wayland was a well-to-do real estate broker in Pueblo, Colorado. But he had become vaguely discontented with what he considered a political and social injustice: a system that benefited entrepreneurs like himself at the expense of less advantaged people. An English shoemaker in Pueblo had introduced him to the essays of the Fabian Society and the social criticism of John Ruskin, and Wayland was beginning his rapid conversion from Republicanism to his own unique blend of enterprising Socialism. Convinced that a depression was coming, he sold his property interests and moved to Greensburg, Indiana, to ride out the storm and prepare to take up again his former craft—printing, publishing, and editing—in behalf of his adopted cause.

Socialism had not surfaced as a mass movement in the United States at that time, but it had a large following in Europe, and it took a multitude of different forms. Karl Marx and Friedrich Engels were the movement's radicals, the proponents of a violent and revolutionary class struggle. The Fabians, whose number included George Bernard Shaw, were opposed to the Marxist theory, holding that more evolutionary social reforms within existing institutions would bring about the natural development of Socialism. The earlier utopian Socialists—principally Robert Owen and Charles Fourier—were idealists who envisioned the creation of communitarian settlements based on voluntary and cooperative sharing of all resources, and their views were carried forward in the last years of the century by other idealists, most notably the English novelist Edward Bellamy. There were also the Christian Socialists, of whom Thomas Hughes was one. And then there was John Ruskin, an English art critic and social theorist whose early writings on art and architecture gave way to more broadly directed social and political criticism and to the advocacy of positive programs for social reform. Many of his theories on such things as old age pensions, publicly financed education, and the organization of labor have long since become accepted principles.

Wayland studied many of Ruskin's works, and he read *Looking Backward,* Bellamy's 1888 novel describing an orderly, problem-free cooperative society of the future. The two Englishmen not only expressed views and ideas he shared enthusiastically; they also wrote with a style and flair he deeply admired. Their skill as writers prompted him to take up his own pen in emulation, and their ideas became the basis for the utopian Socialist community he dreamed of creating. More than any others, Ruskin and Bellamy were the philosophical giants in Wayland's vision of Socialism.

In Indiana, he launched a weekly newspaper on April 29, 1893, naming it *The Coming Nation.* Within six months it had a paid circulation of 13,000 and was completely self-supporting, even though its income was derived entirely from subscriptions (capitalist advertising was not accepted). Wayland wrote most of the copy himself, and the remainder came primarily from reprints of Socialist tracts and the correspondence of the readers. The newspaper revealed much about Wayland himself. It avoided complex theoretical discourses and stuck to simple issues, laid out in short, pithy paragraphs. It contained none of the hair-splitting arguments that divided different kinds of Socialists one from another, but advocated instead a flexible and inclusive philosophy uniting all Socialists against their common enemy: capitalism. Its four pages of aphorisms, one-liners, short editorials, and eye-catching tidbits of information were clearly directed to the masses of common people, not to an intellectual elite. Wayland had little patience with the theoreticians, whose windy arguments bored him; he wanted to popularize Socialism for the benefit of the multitudes of impoverished workers, and an astonishing number of them responded with 50-cents-a-year subscriptions and enthusiastic letters of encouragement. He had the deft touch of an advertising man, a publicist, a promoter—and the hard-hitting delivery of an evangelist. Many of the intellectuals of the movement looked askance at his over-simplifications, but they could only envy his ability to move the multitude.

By the spring of 1894, the circulation of *The Coming Nation* exceeded 50,000. Wayland had been telling his readers that a circulation of 100,000 would produce a surplus of about $23,000 a year, and that the money would be used to buy a tract of land upon which a Socialist colony—"The Co-operative Commonwealth"—would be built. He promised that those who sent in 200 or more subscriptions to the paper, or contributed as much (presumably $100, at the rate of 50 cents per subscription), would be the charter members of the colony. His intent was to create a practical, functioning model of social reform, a demonstration of his faith that cooperation and other Socialist principles were superior to monopoly and competition. By summer, Wayland had become a controversial and unwanted figure in the little town of Greensburg, but he was a popular hero to his far-flung readers; and although the paper's circulation had not reached 100,000, he decided it was time to move. His agents had been searching the interior of the nation for suitable land, concentrating their efforts in Kentucky and Tennessee, and they decided finally upon two adjoining 500-acre tracts at Tennessee City, a small community in Dickson County, about fifty miles west of Nashville. The price was $2,500—$2.50 an acre—and since the property was served by a nearby railroad and post office, both of which the colony would need, Wayland felt he had made a good bargain. In the July 21, 1894, issue of *The Coming Nation*, he sent out a call to the charter members of the new community and announced that the next issue of the paper would come from Tennessee.

The first dozen settlers arrived in the heat of summer, and lived in tents while they cut timber and erected the first structure—a building to house the printing press that was to be their principal source of income. One of them later described Tennessee City as "a sorry collection of primitive Southern homes on a railroad track," with the post office and "a run-down hotel" nearby. The property, which had been owned by a Chicago land company, was pleasing to look at, but its forested hillsides and rocky flatlands yielded stubbornly and sparsely to the new tenants, who struggled under extreme difficulty to gain a foothold.

They were a diverse and interesting assembly from all over the United States. Accounts vary as to their number, but the first group apparently included about twenty men and a dozen women, some of them couples with children, others single. They were, by the standards of the time, middle-class people—city-dwellers, by and large, craftsmen and professionals, intelligent and well-read individuals. The depression had driven them to refuge in Socialism, and the one thing they held in common was a desire to escape from the competitive society and start anew in an atmosphere of cooperation. There was a butcher, a baker, a barber, a blacksmith; there were five printers, three doctors, two ironworkers, and several teachers and farmers. And there was their convenor, Julius Wayland, who named the colony Ruskin, in honor of the man whose "great, loving, wise spirit" had led them there. John Ruskin, he said, was his model, and "his mind is my inspiration."

Ironically, Ruskin was by then a seventy-five-year-old man suffering from intermittent periods of insanity that had become almost continuous. Wayland had faithfully mailed him each issue of *The Coming Nation,* and he wrote to tell him of the colony that had been founded in his name. Subsequently, an autographed and finely-bound copy of Ruskin's complete works was received in the Tennessee community, but the old man whose words had inspired Wayland and his comrades was too ill to take an interest in their efforts.

Tennessee had no law suitable for the incorporation of a town such as the Ruskinites envisioned, but Wayland believed the laws that governed business corporations could be adapted to serve the needs of a cooperative association; and on his initiative, the Ruskin Co-operative Association was incorporated under state law, and a charter was drawn up and signed by the adult members of the community. When it was learned that the law forbade women to be incorporators, the charter was redrawn and signed by twenty men on August 16, 1894.

Thus, Ruskin began as a curious amalgamation of political and social ideas. As a cooperative community, it adhered more closely to the romantic visions of Ruskin and Bellamy and to the earlier endeavors of Robert Owen than it did to Marx's more contemporary brand of revolutionary Communism. As an incorporated entity under Tennessee law, it conformed to the structural requirements of capitalism. Its charter permitted the shareholders collectively to acquire land, to own and operate manufacturing facilities, to build houses, to provide educational and recreational services to members, to insure employees against want, and to promote harmonious social relations on the basis of cooperation; but the colony's principal asset—its publishing house— remained the property of Julius Wayland. These apparent contradictions were destined to cause friction, but in the beginning they mattered little—if, indeed, they were even noticed.

Each charter member received one share of stock in the corporation, regardless of the amount he had actually paid in, and the shares were given a

Although it has appeared on Tennessee maps for at least 75 years, Ruskin, in Dickson County, is no longer a community with a post office. But its main building, Commonwealth House, still stands beyond the rusty superstructure of an old bridge across Yellow Creek.

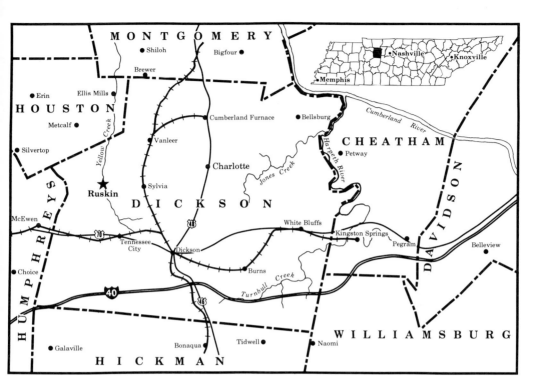

face value of $500 each. Wives as well as husbands received shares, and the
stockholders met once a month to transact the business of the colony. They
elected a board of directors and officers (Wayland was the first president), and
organized the activities of the colony under elected superintendents of education and recreation, agriculture, manufacturing, sanitation and medical care,
public works, cuisine, and distribution. *The Coming Nation* resumed publication from its new plant in August, the settlers worked together to build
individual homes for each family, all meals were provided in a common
dining facility, agricultural and manufacturing activities were initiated, and a
steady stream of new residents came to share in the arduous but productive
undertaking. Under the terms of the charter, each man paid $500 and received
one share of stock when he joined the colony; if he had a wife, she could either
purchase a share of stock for herself or receive the benefits of the community
free of charge, in return for her labor. All work was of equal value. Housing,
food, medical care and other necessities were provided without charge, and
purchases from the community commissary were made with paper certificates, each of which represented one hour of work (a quart of peanuts cost
one hour in scrip, a pound of coffee seven hours, a pair of pants thirty-seven
hours).

Ruskin was organized to the teeth around the principle of cooperation. It
was a place of intense, feverish, exhausting activity, a beehive of zealous and
industrious workers in eager pursuit of a lofty cause, and they generated
enough energy to produce quick and impressive results. In addition to the
printing plant, the houses, and the commissary, they built a kiln and a planing
mill, acquired a herd of dairy cows, and began to manufacture and market
such diverse products as chewing gum, suspenders, and Ruskin Ready Remedy, a cure-all patent medicine priced at 25 cents a bottle. By the fall of 1894,
the colony had almost 100 residents and the newspaper had close to 75,000
subscribers. Wayland told the shareholders in October that he was turning
over to the association "all the material and good-will of *The Coming Nation*,
the building and money." The plant, he said, was worth "at least $50,000,"
although it had a book value of $15,000, most of which belonged to his wife.
(That, incidentally, was one of the few references Wayland ever made to his
marital status.)

In the October 13 edition of *The Coming Nation*, Wayland inserted a brief

*Early photographs of unknown origin show the settlers of Ruskin to be
industrious and enterprising people. When they were building the colony,
they lived in tents and ate outdoors (top). Later, they operated an extensive
canning industry inside Ruskin Cave (bottom).*

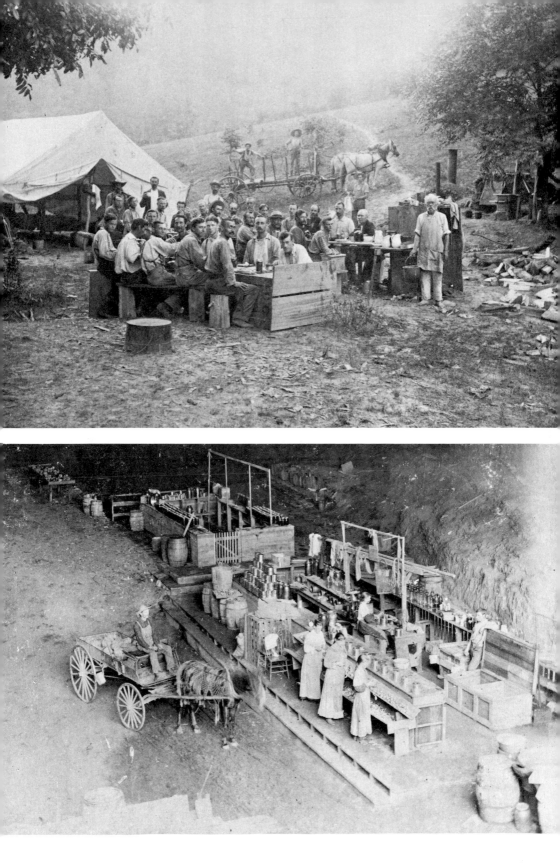

editorial comment which seems in retrospect to suggest that trouble was already brewing beneath the peaceful surface at Ruskin. "There is no danger to our colony from the outside," he wrote. "If our members have sense enough to hold together, not to allow trifling, petty matters to create dissention [*sic*], this colony will grow to rival other corporations and all its members will be rich in all the opportunities of life. I have no fear of outside interference, nor quarrels over weighty matters. It is only the meanest, smallest matters that can create dissension, and I believe some member of every family is well enough posted to avoid these little clashes."

Ruskin's charter members were already outnumbered by newcomers, and each time the population grew, the potential for disagreement increased. There were "trifling, petty matters" aplenty—quarrels over manners and morals and religious beliefs, and especially over variations of the Socialist theme. Wayland was a non-partisan Socialist, an independent rather than a party loyalist. He fashioned his own doctrine as he went along, and stubbornly held to it in spite of the criticisms of his companions. Impatient of narrowness, he was himself narrow-minded and defensive of his own views, which he felt were broad enough to include everybody and thus should be accepted with deference. But many residents, particularly newcomers, would not defer to him. The press was the big money-maker, and it was spreading the gospel of Socialism far and wide; but Wayland was attacked for running it as a profit-making enterprise, and for controlling it by himself. He defended its prosperity as the life-blood of the colony, yet even after he gave its assets to the association, his opponents called him an individualist and an anarchist—the worst imaginable epithet to any self-respecting Socialist—and accused him of lining his own pockets with money from the newspaper. He attempted to retain editorial control of the paper, but the residents insisted that it be run in the same way that everything else at Ruskin was run—cooperatively.

Throughout the winter and spring of 1895, the running battle between Wayland and his detractors continued, and while the unsuspecting readers of *The Coming Nation* were given only glowing accounts of Ruskin's progress and the march of Socialism, the founder and editor of the paper gradually lost his control of it. Finally, in the middle of the summer, Wayland gave up. His resignation, the paper announced, was "by mutual consent," but in fact he departed in bitter disillusionment, his dream of a model community in shambles. The land he had bought and the printing empire he had created remained

The Ruskin Co-operative Association issued certificates of stock to its settler-owners (top). In place of money, members of the community traded in paper scrip based on units of labor (bottom). A pound of coffee, for example, cost seven hours in scrip.

Series B. No. 1   One Share.

Certificate of Stock.

The Ruskin Co=operative Association.

In pursance of Sections 3, 4 and 5 of Article II. of the By-Laws of Ruskin Co-operative Association, as said Sections appear on the Minutes of the Directors of the Ruskin Co-operative Association of January 12th, 1898, and in consideration of the contract between *Allen Fields* and his wife *Laura E. Fields*, which contract is a part of this certificate of stock, and is especially referred to; and for the further consideration of the sum of $500.00 paid to the said Association, the Ruskin Co-operative Association issues to Mrs. *Laura E. Fields* **One share of stock of the Ruskin Co=operative Association.**

This stock can be held only by Mrs. *Laura E. Fields*; is non-dividend paying, and non-transferable; is not subject to the indebtedness of Mrs. *Laura E. Fields* or her husband, and upon her death or her severance of connection with the said Association, or when she leaves it, the same shall revert immediately to the Ruskin Co-operative Association.

Under it she has all the other rights of a share-holder except as above stated.

In witness whereof the President and Secretary have hereunto subscribed their names at Ruskin, Tennessee, this *24th* day of *March* 1899

B. F. Hunter
Secretary.

Allen Fields
President.

This Certifies that the Bearer has Performed
Five Hours' Labor
For the
Ruskin Co=operative Ass'n.
This Certificate is redeemable in Labor or the Products of Labor in the keeping of the Association, but not in Cash And it is good only when presented by a member of said Association, a prospective member, or a member of their families.
Sec'y.   Pres.
5 HOURS

This Certifies that the Bearer has Performed
Ten Hours' Labor
For the
Ruskin Co=operative Ass'n.
This Certificate is redeemable in Labor or the Products of Labor in the keeping of the Association, but not in Cash And it is good only when presented by a member of said Association, a prospective member, or a member of their families.
Sec'y.   Pres.
10 HOURS

This Certifies that the Bearer has Performed
Three Hours' Labor
For the
Ruskin Co=operative Ass'n.
This Certificate is redeemable in Labor or the Products of Labor in the keeping of the Association, but not in Cash And it is good only when presented by a member of said Association, a prospective member, or a member of their families.
Sec'y.   Pres.
3 HOURS

This Certifies that the Bearer has Performed
Two Hours' Labor
For the
Ruskin Co=operative Ass'n.
This Certificate is redeemable in Labor or the Products of Labor in the keeping of the Association, but not in Cash And it is good only when presented by a member of said Association, a prospective member, or a member of their families.
Sec'y.   Pres.
2 HOURS

in the hands of the association—they were, in fact, its primary assets—yet some of his enemies who called themselves "loyalists to the cause of Socialism" asserted that he left owing the stockholders $3,500.

In truth, he did not leave empty-handed, or so it seems. Within a month, he had launched a new paper, *Appeal to Reason,* in Kansas City; and he had enough resources to see it through a money-losing year there before moving the operation to Girard, Kansas, where it became a vastly successful publication and the leading Socialist newspaper in America. Wayland was to meet again with *The Coming Nation* under circumstances that could only have given him a satisfying feeling of vindication, but his departure from Ruskin was anything but triumphant. Historian Robert Corlew called it "another case of Jerusalem stoning her prophets." Wayland had written in one issue of *The Coming Nation* that each stockholder owned one share of non-assessable, non-dividend-paying, non-proxy-voting, non-transferable stock, "and it will be to you of no value, except as it gives you the right to be one of us." When he became a minority of one, that prophetic declaration applied to him, and he gave up his valueless share of stock and left in disgrace and defiance.

Ruskin did not collapse after Wayland left. The stockholders, who had gained complete control of the newspaper, turned the editorship of it over to Alfred S. Edwards, a former associate of Wayland's who had parted company with him after a disagreement. The circulation of *The Coming Nation* held steady, and the population of Ruskin continued to grow, and late in 1895 the colony demonstrated its vitality in a daring move. Having found their land unsuitable for agricultural production, the Ruskinites decided to buy additional property in the vicinity and to move the entire enterprise—houses, printing plant and all—to the new site.

The land was located five miles north of Tennessee City, in the fertile valley of Yellow Creek. It had, in addition to abundant timber, limestone, and brick clay, 300 acres of arable land and two enormous caves, one of which was used as a meeting place and a natural refrigerator for food storage. In all, the colonists acquired about 800 acres at an average of $20 an acre, paying about half of the $16,000 purchase price in cash and mortgaging the rest, using their Tennessee City property as collateral. The move was made in stages over a year's time, and by the beginning of 1897, it was complete: Ruskin had a new home, at the center of which was Commonwealth House, an imposing three-story structure housing the printery, the communal dining room, lodging for newcomers and visitors, a nursery, a bookstore, and a library. It was a huge, barn-like building that towered above the crude houses of the colonists, and on its third floor, in an auditorium large enough for 700 seats, plays and lectures and musical programs were staged, and art exhibits lined the walls. In the less rarefied atmosphere at ground level, buildings that had been moved from the old site were placed with houses, barns, a blacksmith shop, and a store that had been there before; and the aggregate gave Ruskin all the essential elements of a thriving and prosperous town. The first part of 1897 may have been the colony's zenith. It had assets of close to $100,000, made up of 1,800 acres of land, a highly successful newspaper and printing business, no less than seventy-five buildings, a diversified agricultural operation, a sawmill, a grist mill, a steam laundry, a machine shop, a cafe, a bakery, a school, a commissary, a cannery, and several cottage industries whose products were advertised and sold by mail and across the counter. Ruskin also had about 250 residents who had come from thirty-two states and half a dozen foreign countries, and they worked nine hours a day at whatever jobs they agreed to perform, receiving in scrip the equivalent of $5 a week for their efforts. Ostensibly, the principles of Socialism were resoundingly successful. Once-hostile neighbors had begun to admire the industriousness of the Ruskinites, to trade with them, and even on occasion to socialize with them. The Nashville *Banner* called the colony "a commendable and harmless enterprise." To observers on the outside, Ruskin seemed to have arrived and conquered.

But it was within two years of total collapse. Its problems, as Wayland had said they would be, were internal, and they were multiple and complex. A change in the by-laws gave the board of directors complete control over all the affairs of the association, and stockholder meetings, which had been held once a month, became pro-forma, once-a-year affairs. A women's rights dispute developed between the wives of charter members, each of whom owned a voting share in the corporation, and the women who had arrived later, most of whom had no share and thus no vote. The division between charter members and the other colonists had grown from a narrow fissure to a gaping chasm, and when the charter members sought an injunction from a Dickson County court to prevent the issuance of stock to "non-charter" women unless they paid the $500 fee, there was no repairing the damage. What had been a private dispute behind closed doors became an open conflict involving the law and the courts, and that change signaled the beginning of Ruskin's demise.

There was a pronounced division between the charter members and most of those who came after them. For the most part, the original colonists were middle-class urbanites with an intellectual and philosophical interest in Socialism. They were not radicals but romantics, gentle people who believed in the principle of cooperation but opposed the theory of the class struggle. They worked hard for themselves and for the community, and in their shared achievements and failures they quickly became a close-knit group. The later arrivals often found it difficult to enter that first circle, for a number of reasons. Many of them came from rural areas, or from the hard-hit ranks of the depressed working class. Some were unhappy with the limited choice of jobs available, other resented the notion of cooperation and sharing, and a few were loafers and freeloaders. They were, as a group, less disciplined, less well educated, and more radical than their predecessors. They sensed an attitude of superiority among the charter members—a feeling that was reinforced by some who expressed the view that a higher value should be placed on "brain" work and "thinking" jobs than on "hand" work and common labor.

Out of this sharp separation arose several conflicts. Some of the charter members who helped to oust Wayland because he refused to share control of the press found themselves under attack for their reluctance to share power with the newer members. Admission to the colony was made more difficult—a preliminary visit was required, as was a written examination on the principles of cooperation and Socialism, in addition to the $500 fee and approval of a majority of the stockholders—but the restrictions failed to lessen the dissension, and a few people moved into the community without ever becoming members.

Education was another bone of contention. From the beginning, great emphasis had been placed on the school program, and on cultural and intellectual activities for all ages, as well as on the teaching of Socialist principles. But as time passed the interest began to diminish, and educational pursuits were given a lower priority. When the colony was relocated at the cave site, twenty-five acres were set aside for the Ruskin College of the New Economy, and a resident architect designed a building for it. Money was raised through appeals in *The Coming Nation,* and in June of 1897 a ceremony was held for the laying of a cornerstone, but the building was never completed and the college was never opened. By then, the Ruskinites had other things on their minds.

The colonists also had serious quarrels about religion. There was no church in the village, the residents at first being indifferent to religion. Later, a Sunday School was organized to meet in private homes, and some colonists went outside the community to church., In time, the membership included some who practiced spiritualism and healing faith, others who came from the major Protestant denominations, and still others who were militantly anti-

With the latest in printing equipment (insert), the Ruskinites published The Coming Nation, *their newspaper devoted to "the Common Ownership of All Means of Production and Distribution." By the beginning of 1895, the paper had 75,000 subscribers scattered across the United States.*

Coming Nation

RUSKIN, TENN., SATURDAY, SEPTEMBER 11, 1897.

This Paper Stands for the Common Ownership of All Means of Production and Distribution, and is Edited and Published in a Co-operative Community Based on that Principle.

SEVENOAKS.

Who Are "We the People?"

CONSIDERED numerically, "we the people" are about twenty millions, in round numbers, and we are the people because the double privilege of working and voting is ours. Outside of our twenty millions of workers and voters, and, by the way, the workers don't always work, because they have no country, and the voters don't always vote, because voting is credited with an efficiency than their own experience confirms—but outside of we twenty millions who work part of the time and vote as long as we are through we googgle darkly, we have a million capitalists who, not working themselves control the destinies of those who do, and not voting themselves, manufacture the vote and the results of voting. "We the people," although we do all the useful work that is done and cast all the useless votes that a ballot box, permit an organized million, one-twentieth of our number, to appropriate the hard fruits of our toil, live in luxury, dictate our laws, our government, and decide what measure of life, liberty and happiness escapes from the cradle to the coffin. We, twenty millions of us, attract a land that once had one king and now has fifty, vainly imagining that free and boasting that we are sovereigns, when all the while most of us possess slaves; "we the people" scrupulously respecting the right of a million lawfully or unlawfully to exact from us rents, interest, profits, taxes for their own benefit. We twenty millions, or thereabouts, trickled believing that it is a childish to believe that we shall avoid 'shipwreck...

HELP THE STRIKING MINERS.

The St. Louis Meeting---Labor Leaders Declare for Collective Ownership of Mines and Transportation---Dispatch From Eugene Debs--- National Gathering Called for September 27.

[SPECIAL TO THE COMING NATION.]

ST. LOUIS, Aug. 31.—The convention has adjourned after two days of hard work...

EUGENE V. DEBS.

ENDURANCE OF THE TOILERS.

EXTRACT FROM A SPEECH BY M. JAURES, THE FRENCH SOCIALIST DEPUTY.

BY WHAT virtue have the toilers been able to endure their eternal life of nakedness and privation? For eighteen hundred years, under the powerful organization of the Roman Gauls, under the triumph of the feudal system, under the grasping bourgeoisie, they have seen flowing out to others the fountains of riches which they had made to leap forth from the soil. For them the toil of suntime beneath the heavy sun, for them the fierce struggle of the ax with the oak, for them the short sleep in stables and the waking from the earliest hours, sixteen of the day, to the harsh cares of their cattle. But it is always to the noble Gaul, proud that he has journeyed to Rome, to the feudal knight in harness for the tournament, to the bourgeois and the rich financier, that, from century to century, have gone the wealth of the vineyards and the fields, the strength of the summers, the plenty of autumn—it is always for others that they wear themselves out and suffer.

By pushing back competition from one point we only succeed in multiplying it in every other. In this tossing, dying whirlpool it would be childish to believe that we shall avoid 'shipwreck by thrusting a single plank into the water. * * * Our time is fertile in wonderful reactions. It is like an immense keyboard, whose resonance is unforeseen and far away. * * * With protectionism the misery of the peasant is not near its end.

Yet, these long years of suffering will not have been lost sufferings to him. * * * Behold, his labor remains barren; the price of his corn and wine and oil depends no longer on rain or frost; and he has the feeling that all these variations have for their cause a human fact, a social phenomenon. From every side, statesmen, financiers, economists, deputies and candidates to parliament make answer to him that for half a century humanity has worked the earth as he has done; that in the great plains of Russia, of India, of Western America, other men work as he does, but at less expense, and that all this far-off production brought near by rapid transport weighs upon his own. And so, for him, far-off peoples and continents rise up from out the mists, no longer like the itself ... phantoms of a schoolboy's geography, but like harsh and massive realities. And they add that, perhaps, on the question of the wheat harvested in America, on the gold and silver dug out in South Africa, on the wages distributed among the day laborers of India, on the customs duties promulgated in all the countries of the world, shall depend for him tomorrow the price of his corn and perhaps his liberty, perhaps his property?

SPECIAL EDITION.

The issue of THE COMING NATION for September 25 will be a Special Edition, containing articles by representative labor leaders of the United States on "Collective Ownership of Mines..."

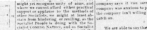

pality has established a fund for advancing loans to the students on honor and without security or interest.

"If you can, with the law's help, rob a workingman of his home, you are 'successful.'"

"If you can embezzle the funds of a ...

We are able to say that Socialism is pretty well planted in the United States army—among both officers and men.

religious. Emotional religious conflicts sometimes erupted, and they were seldom tempered with brotherly love.

Finally, the most visible and outwardly controversial dispute was about sex. A few of the latecomers to Ruskin were advocates of "free love" and against marriage, and their well-publicized arguments with the monogamous colonists created in the minds of many outsiders a false impression of rampant immorality. The "free love" dispute was actually a minor matter concerning only a few Ruskinites, but it was magnified out of all proportion to its importance, and it became yet another strain on the already weakened cord that bound Ruskin together.

The colony's internal unraveling seemed to begin just when its external image was becoming favorable. Ruskin was in sound financial condition, with no debts outstanding except the property mortgage. Its members paid their poll taxes and road taxes, and in 1896 they voted four-to-one in favor of the Democratic-Populist candidate for President, William Jennings Bryan, as did their Dickson County neighbors. The county school system paid Ruskin $2 per pupil for the operation of a five-month school, and the colony kept school in session ten months a year and provided the building and teachers. And after the Ruskinites had served free barbecue to 2,000 people at a public Fourth of July celebration in the big cave in 1896, a newspaper in Waverly praised the colonists as "not anarchists and revolutionaries but good, law-abiding citizens whom any county would be glad to claim."

By the middle of 1897, Ruskin's internal crisis was building rapidly. Some insiders complained that it was "not Socialist enough." Others said its affairs were controlled by "a secret ring," and it had become "a closed corporation for a favored few." Charges and countercharges of "capitalism" and "anarchy" and "individualism" were tossed about. It was asserted that the colony had no discipline and no leadership. Politics, religion, and sex—three eternally unresolvable subjects of debate—were endlessly debated. There was no willingness to compromise, and cooperation had become nothing more than a word in the name of the association. Any who think Ruskin is a paradise, a columnist in *The Coming Nation* wrote, "get a wrong idea of our colony. We are but human, with 5,000 years of inherited prejudices. . . . We can't change human nature in four years." That oblique acknowledgment was about as close as the newspaper ever came to reporting on Ruskin's problems.

But the problems continued. In June 1897, three colonists preparing to resign from the community turned in their shares of stock and asked for a $500 refund. The colony leaders had honored such requests in the past as a matter of policy, but they refused the three men, explaining that the local constable had come to collect on bad debts they had incurred, and their shares had been sold to pay their creditors. The men promptly sued the colony, and subsequently were countersued for libel. The resort to court action had been tried once again, and in the coming months it would be tried many more times.

Early in 1898, a group of dissidents agreed to leave the colony if their $500 shares were redeemed, but some of the men claimed full shares for their wives as well as themselves, and the dispute over equal rights for women surfaced once more. Altogether, nine court injunctions were sought in 1898 and 1899. Somehow, Ruskin kept going, but its population had stopped growing and the circulation of *The Coming Nation* had begun to drop. The colonists were in court almost as often as they were at work, and their constant preoccupation was not Socialism but survival. As the months dragged on, the collapse of the colony seemed more and more certain.

The end almost came in May of 1899. A small group of colonists, most of them charter members, went into court and sought to have the Ruskin corporation dissolved. The judge denied their motion, saying they lacked sufficient evidence to prove their assets in the corporation were being squandered. But the law did give the court broad discretion in cases concerning the rights of stockholders, and it was clear that the colony might be vulnerable to a call for liquidation by a few dissatisfied shareowners. Under the deteriorating circumstances, the tactic seemed bound to succeed eventually.

By then only a small handful of charter members remained at Ruskin, and they had few allies in their campaign to have the colony dissolved. A majority of the stockholders held a closed meeting in secret and decided that liquidation might indeed be the best strategy, as long as they controlled it. They voted to abolish the Ruskin Co-operative Association, and to create a new entity, the Ruskin Commonwealth. Their plan was to ask the court to sell the assets of the association and to distribute the proceeds among its members, who could then choose to remain in the newly formed Ruskin Commonwealth or leave. But the charter group—the minority—learned of the plan and beat the majority to the punch. At their urging, a judge declared the colony hopelessly deadlocked and appointed a receiver to sell the assets at auction.

It seems of little consequence now which side initiated the action, since, in effect, both factions had concluded that liquidation was inevitable. But in the heat and emotion of the time, every move seemed to have an exaggerated importance in the minds of all the colonists, and even predictable and expected developments caused shock and excitement. More than thirty years after Ruskin failed, a former colonist named J. T. McDill recalled the moment when the fateful news reached him. "Our little Eden was not to last," he wrote. "I was out in the field with a hoe when the news came. A receiver had been appointed to sell us out for technical violations of the anti trust laws. The decision was final. There was no appeal.'' The sale was set for June, and then postponed to July 26.

McDill was not a charter member, and it is not altogether clear which camp he was in. The same apparently can be said for many other colonists. They were not always well informed about the various intrigues that were afoot, and they sometimes aligned themselves differently from one issue to the next. Ruskin was seldom if ever divided sharply into two rigidly defined ideological factions; it could more accurately be described as a collection of shifting coalitions, the shape and strength of which often changed. And on the issue of liquidation, there turned out to be three factions: the charter minority, who got the injunction; the majority, who formed the new Ruskin Commonwealth; and a group of about thirty people, described by a Nashville newspaper reporter as the ''cream'' of the colonists, who were making their own individual plans for the future.

Only 138 stockholding members remained at Ruskin. Theoretically, each one stood to receive par value—$500—for his or her share, and since the assets of the colony had been valued at $94,000 in a January 1899 inventory, most of them hoped and expected to receive at least par value, and perhaps more. But they were naïve about the arcane complexities of the law and the courts. A forced sale, they were told, would not yield anything like the true value of the properties, and there would be court costs and legal fees and mortgages to settle. Furthermore, the circulation of *The Coming Nation* had fallen from 60,000 to 11,000, reducing its worth accordingly. They might be lucky to realize $250 apiece.

In part to build the community's assets and in part as a farewell gesture to their neighbors, the Ruskinites managed to reach an agreement on one thing: they would invite the public to one last Fourth of July celebration at the cave. It was a grand and heartwarming affair. The colonists put many of their personal belongings on sale, as well as the products of their industries, and they provided music and entertainment and generous amounts of barbecue and ice cream. They sold admission tickets for 25 cents apiece, and although the day's attendance was estimated to be 1,500 people, about 5,000 tickets were sold. Recalled J. T. McDill in 1932: ''They bought everything we had to sell, [and those who] had some money left threw it all in a hat and donated it to us.'' He and many others were overwhelmed: '' . . . those grand people . . . rallied to support and comfort us. . . . We had outraged their religious beliefs.

Julius Augustus Wayland, the founder of Ruskin, was 54 years old when this photograph was taken in 1908, thirteen years after he left the Tennessee colony. The original of the photograph belongs to his son, Walter Wayland, of Girard, Kansas.

We had reviled their politics. We had mocked their simplicity. And they forgave all.'' It was Ruskin's last happy day.

The sale and its aftermath were a disaster for the colonists. Hundreds of people came looking for bargains, and they found them: fine horses sold for as little as $10, mules for $9, hogs for $5. The original 1,000-acre property at Tennessee City, which Julius Wayland had bought in 1894 for $2,500, attracted a high bid of $2,300. The thirty or so colonists who sided neither with the majority nor with the charter group decided they wanted the cave site for a non-ideological community of private homes, and their representative bid $11,000 for the 800-acre site that had been purchased three years earlier for $16,000 and was still encumbered by a mortgage of almost $6,000. Considering improvements and higher land costs, both parcels were probably worth more than the high bids, but under the circumstances, the prices seemed satisfactory. To the chagrin of the colonists, however, both deals fell through when the high bidders could not raise enough money to take possession. An involved legal hassle ensued, and the sale was reopened. When it was all over, a man named Thomas Rogers—possibly the same individual who had sold the colonists a 384-acre section of the cave site for $10,500 in 1896—was declared the high bidder on the entire 1,800-acre Ruskin property. He got it all for a grand total of $1,505. The mortgages on the land were left for the colonists to pay from their receipts.

All in all, the assets of Ruskin brought in about $16,500. Settlement of the mortgages reduced that amount to $10,600. Court costs, the claims of creditors, and the fees of the receivers and the attorneys took another $5,200 or so, leaving about $5,400 to be divided 138 ways. Each colonist got approximately $39 and a little change.

The members of the new Ruskin Commonwealth pooled their resources to buy *The Coming Nation* and its presses and joined with a group of Indiana Socialists who had bought a tract of land seven miles south of Waycross, Georgia. They moved there in October of 1899 and started a new colony, resuming publication of the newspaper. Their little post office at the village of Duke, on the edge of the Okefenokee Swamp, was renamed Ruskin on January 1, 1900, but the colonizing venture was short-lived. In less than eighteen months, it had succumbed to hot weather, fire, sickness, suspicious neighbors, and poor credit. The local sheriff sold the printing equipment in February 1901 to cover bad debts. (The Ruskin place name, however, can still be found on Georgia road maps.)

Ruskin was finally finished. The New York *Journal* editorialized that the association ''was perfectly solvent,'' and its failure was ''not commercial.'' Its problems, the paper said, had been caused by ''the dissatisfaction of less than a dozen members.'' Others were less charitable, saying ''bums and

hoboes'' made a poor mix with ''well-educated and cultured people.'' A
daughter of one of the colonists said later that Ruskin had attempted ''to carry
out one economic order in a limited sphere, while surrounded by and under the
general laws of an entirely different economic order.'' It was not a question of
which was right or best, she said, but of ''the impossibility of coexistence
between irreconcilible systems.''

Isaac Broome, who had joined the Ruskin community in about 1896, wrote
a book in 1902 called *The Last Days of the Ruskin Co-operative Association*.
It is full of sarcasm and bitterness about the fall of what to him was a
high-minded and highly promising venture. In his view, Julius Wayland was a
genius and most of the earliest settlers were sincere and dedicated people.
Many of the latecomers, he said, were undisciplined, ill-mannered, ignorant
anarchists. He mentioned in particular a man named Cowell, a printer, who
never became a member of the colony but who led the ''free love anarchists''
and caused general disruption and conflict throughout his brief stay.

By coincidence, the same Cowell is mentioned prominently in a manuscript
written by W. L. Cook in about 1920. At the time of the Ruskin controversy,
Cook was a young lawyer in Charlotte, the seat of Dickson County (he later
served on the Tennessee Supreme Court). In his written recollection he
described how three young strangers—one of them Cowell—came to his
office to seek legal advice:

> They came to employ a lawyer and said they had been sent to me; that
> they had no patience with the law, had no respect for the law, no confidence
> in the integrity of courts, and had no desire to seek protection from the
> State, but since they were forced by circumstances beyond their control to
> be denizens of earth in this benighted age when silly men sustained legal
> institutions, they supposed it would be advisable to employ counsel who
> might succeed in keeping their affairs measurably within the law. They
> were careful to impress that they did not believe in lawsuits, and would not
> engage in litigation.

> They profoundly impressed my young mind as the emissaries from a
> dreamland, who in the slow march toward human perfection had sprinted
> ahead, reached the goal, outdistanced civilization, outrun Christianity,
> given the lie to evolution, and entered into the millenium ahead of schedule
> time. In contemplating their speed it seemed that by comparison the winner
> of the Derby was as slow as the hundred to one shot that never left the post.

The three men hired Cook to represent their interests in the event the colony
was liquidated. Since it is known that Cowell left Ruskin in the fall of 1897, it
can be inferred from the Cook manuscript that legal dissolution of the
corporation was being discussed long before it was actually tried. In any
event, Cook's jaundiced view of the colony led him to write:

The community went to pieces quicker because Cowell and others were there. It would have gone to pieces sooner or later, because the very plan of the organization left no outlet for individual expression. Everyone had to breathe through the Community quill; every one had to eat Community bread; everyone had to swill Community soup. Five hundred tastes were compelled to fit their appetites to the cook's idea of diet, and his idea was limited by the necessities of the Community and its means of meeting them. No one was satisfied, and his only remedy was to leave and carry nothing with him, or to grumble. There was grumbling enough.

What a pity Human Nature denied the dreamers sleep. By now the property which had been acquired by the Community at the time of its dissolution, in consequence of accretion, their effort, and the advance in prices would have reached near a million dollars in value. And more, under the inspiration of their environment, the families of the members might have developed a new vision, a new culture, and might have become home loving individualists, here among these hills, and trees and flowers.

Cook wrote in another passage that there were "several clean men and women" among the Ruskin colonists, "along with a lot of nuts, anarchists, and nondescripts." Another early resident of the neighboring countryside classified them all as "Communists," and "a wicked bunch." Both assessments seem excessive. It is doubtful that more than a small minority of colonists ever seriously supported the tenets of Marxism, and fewer still lived in such a way as to justify being called "a wicked bunch." As for the "nuts, anarchists, and nondescripts," their number may have been more than a few, but the available evidence strongly indicates that throughout its short life, Ruskin had more "clean men and women"—decent, well-meaning, industrious people—than any other kind.

The colonists scattered after the sale—and later, after the Georgia experiment folded—and in a short time they were as widely separated as they had been when Julius Wayland summoned them to Tennessee. About a dozen of them went together to a "single tax" colony at Fairhope, Alabama, and others joined utopian communities in California and elsewhere. A substantial number remained in the vicinity of Ruskin, including W. H. Charlesworth, a physician, and W. H. Lawson, a newspaper pressman and stereotyper. Another Ruskinite, J. T. McDill, moved to Nashville and served as secretary of the Socialist Party in Tennessee. For a time, he also published a newspaper, *The Ruskin Bugle* ("Subscription Price, Nothing Per Year"), the sole purpose of which was to keep the far-flung former colonists in touch with one another. These excerpts from the April 1906 edition reveal both ordinary and extraordinary qualities in the lives of some of the colony's erstwhile citizens:

From Mr. and Mrs. Robert Jardin in Ruskin: "Down the creek Dodge and

McLane are 'batching' it at the chicken farm, with the chicken house for a composing room and Rhode's house for a press room. They are starting a colony, but I don't know how they are making out. The Lawsons are all living in Washington now. Mr. Lawson has a position as superintendent of a printing department in the treasury building, printing internal revenue stamps. Charlesworth is at Carlisle, Tennessee, practicing medicine. Rosselle was in Jacksonville, Florida, the last I heard. Malcomb Rosselle is coxswain on the U.S. Ship Cincinnati. Rogers is in Memphis, connected in some way with the axhandle business."

From Hattie Schofield in White Springs, Florida: "Walter is working at the carpenter trade, getting $1.25 a day."

From Mary Rhode in Cleveland, Ohio: "Gust. and Con. Doll are working at the Eberhard Malleable Iron Works. Wages are pretty good and work pretty hard. Otto works in a bar fixture shop and Albert is teaming for a brick company. Pa is making new shoes for a company. I'm a milliner, but at present am working at home. With our family we are seldom out of work. As for our prospects, what prospects do wage earners ever have? I suppose it is very much the same with all of them. There is one thing which the boys are doing which I must mention and that is, working for Socialism."

From J. E. Chase in Big Stone County, Minnesota: "We are still paying rent for the blessed privilege of working a half section of worn-out land, but if we are blessed with prosperity we will cut it out in a short time and see if we can't find a few acres of God's green earth that we can call our own."

From Victor Mardfin in New York City: "Pop met Dan Nevinger in the subway a few days ago and he is coming to see us. At present he is working as a carpenter. The Dimmicks live in Brooklyn. Mr. Casson [the last editor of *The Coming Nation* in Tennessee] is connected with *Munsey's Magazine*. I notice in *The Bugle* that Archie McDill has joined the church. I joined the Y.M.C.A. and soon absorbed enough of their teaching to come out as a full-fledged Christian. Mr. Casson told me that my religion was like the measles, 'very easily caught and soon passes away.' It turned out that way."

The letters read like a personals column in a country newspaper, and they further weaken the argument that the Ruskin rank and file was a revolutionary—or even a radical—community.

One other man who lived in the Tennessee colony should be mentioned. His name was Walter Van Fleet. He was a retired physician from New Jersey, and he went to Ruskin in 1897, not so much to practice medicine as to pursue his avocation: horticulture. At some time in his life—whether before or after Ruskin, it is not clear—he apparently directed the rose division of the U.S. Department of Agriculture. When the colony was dissolved, he went back to

New Jersey, but he left his signature behind in the abundant blooming gardens along the bank of Yellow Creek. And today, his signature is also on a fragrant pink climbing rose which he bred and developed: the Van Fleet Rose.

In 1904, a conservative religious denomination bought the cave property where Ruskin had been and opened a college there—Ruskin Cave College— and in Commonwealth House, the great hall that had been the center of the Socialist colony, hymn-singing and preaching echoed through the auditorium, and a painting of Jesus took the place of John Ruskin's portrait. Ruskin might well have been pleased by that; he had memorized the Bible as a boy, and had prepared for the ministry, and some of his social criticism in later life reflected what he might have called the "radical Socialism" of Jesus.

The college lasted about twenty years, and after it closed, Ruskin became almost a ghost town. Today, it is a privately-owned recreation center and summer playground. Commonwealth House, the only remaining original building of any importance, stands gray and empty in the summer shade, and there is a swimming pool near the creek, and square dances are held on a planked floor in the cool mouth of Ruskin Cave. During most of the year, not much happens at Ruskin. But on one day—the Fourth of July—people seem to appear from out of nowhere to celebrate the birth of the American Republic in much the same way as a little band of Socialists and their neighbors did three-quarters of a century ago.

One loose thread in the Ruskin story remains to be tied. Julius Wayland was editing his Socialist newspaper, *Appeal to Reason,* in Girard, Kansas, when he learned that *The Coming Nation* had been dissolved and sold in Georgia. He sent a representative to buy it, and it was subsequently merged with his highly successful Kansas enterprise. Doctrinaire radicals in the Socialist Party apparently thought little of Wayland and his shoot-from-the-hip brand of Socialism, but his readers obviously liked him, and so did Eugene V. Debs, who wrote a column for the paper. Wayland was a man of many contradictions: a believer in political action but not a party loyalist, a utopian who lost his faith in colonization schemes, a soft-hearted man with a hot temper, and finally, an eternal optimist who committed suicide.

Shortly before his death, when Ruskin was a faded memory and *The Coming Nation* had been given a decent burial in the pages of *Appeal to Reason,* it must have become clear to Julius Wayland that Debs would never be President and the coming nation would not be Socialist. In an unguarded moment of candor, he spoke his own epitaph: "The struggle against the capitalist system isn't worth it. Let it pass." And he did.

5. Reflections on Utopianism

It has been estimated that upwards of 200 experimental utopian communities were started in the United States during the 1800s, and that guess is probably on the low side. The times were right for such endeavors: when the century began, the Union had sixteen states and five million people; when it ended, there were forty-five states and seventy-six million people. The entire nation was still an experimental community in 1800, and in the next 100 years it went through the exploration and settlement of its frontiers, fought a series of external and internal wars, and experienced a continuous evolution in its economic and political system. The existence of so many utopias during that period can be seen as an indication of people's dissatisfaction with the way things were at a given time; they are also a reflection of the vitality and optimism of people who dared to start over time and time again in the search for ways to improve the social contract.

The origin of the word utopia is Greek; its literal meaning is "no place." The implication is that utopias are romantic and idealistic visions that cannot exist in the realistic world. It is certainly true that no perfect social order has been devised, and given the fallibility of the human species, none is apt to be. But the continuous striving for perfection has not been fruitless; on the contrary, it has contributed new ideas and a spirit of perpetual renewal to the history of this nation, which has in its Constitution an idealistic and near-utopian objective: "to form a more perfect Union." The functional meaning of utopia, therefore, is not a perfect place, but the aspiration to create one; it is oriented to the future rather than to the past or the present, and its virtue is not in what it has achieved but in what it is willing to attempt.

The three nineteenth-century Tennessee utopias highlighted here had some similarities and some differences, both among themselves and in comparison with others of the same period. Their differences are perhaps most obvious: Nashoba was ostensibly intended to provide American slaves with freedom and equality; Rugby to provide English immigrants with economic and vocational opportunity; and Ruskin to provide disaffected Americans with a

new political and social system. The three colonies also differed in their
methods of financing and in their internal decision-making procedures.

But they also had some striking similarities:

• Each of the three was initiated by a single individual who had an idealistic
vision, a strong personality, and a large public following.

• Each of the communities was established in Tennessee almost by accident—not as a conscious choice of a favorable environment, but as an
incidental choice of available land.

• Each was developed as a cooperative community emphasizing shared
assets and shared responsibility, and each borrowed from the social and
economic ideas of Robert Owen, the British-born reformer whose experimental community at New Harmony, Indiana, was one of the earliest and most
influential utopian colonies in the United States.

• For all their knowledge of Robert Owen and his philosophy of cooperation, the three founders apparently had no knowledge at all of the experimental colonies which preceded them in Tennessee. There is nothing in the record
to indicate that Frances Wright ever heard of Christian Priber's Kingdom of
Paradise, or that Thomas Hughes ever heard of Nashoba, or even that Julius
Wayland was aware of Rugby—though it still existed when Ruskin began.

• Each of the three colonies suffered from a lack of strong resident leadership in the absence of its founder, and internal mismanagement was a major
factor in the eventual collapse of all three.

• With the exception of Wayland, the creators of the three communities
were Britishers who criticized economic and social conditions in Europe and
praised America as a land of opportunity. Wayland himself was an American
critical of conditions in his own country, but the inspiration for his experimental colony also came from Europe, particularly from Englishmen such as John
Ruskin, Edward Bellamy, and Robert Owen.

• The three colonies were weakened by a confusion of purposes and
objectives, and their failure to state priorities and stick to them resulted in
faulty selection of settlers, internal dissension, and ultimately in failure.

• Finally, the three communities were made up of people who seem in
retrospect to have been poorly suited for the monumental tasks they under-
took. They had had no experience in community-building; they knew nothing
of the surrounding countryside and the local citizenry; in each instance, they
found the realities of day-to-day living more arduous and more complex than
they had imagined.

In a sense, Nashoba, Rugby, and Ruskin failed spectacularly. Frances
Wright and Thomas Hughes and Julius Wayland received heavy criticism for
those failures, and the public ridicule and condemnation of them and their

idealistic endeavors followed them to the grave. They were dreamers, vision-aries, romantics—and such people seldom receive the honor they deserve. To be sure, they were not as great as their dreams, and their failures were perhaps inevitable from the beginning. But in the light of history, they can be judged less harshly than their contemporaries judged them. The basic instincts which compelled them to try to achieve seemingly impossible feats were sound and correct and commendable instincts. They should be remembered now not for having failed spectacularly, but for having dreamed impossible dreams, and for having tried to make them come true.

More Resources on Tennessee's New Communities

Most of the research for this book on utopian communities in Tennessee depended upon two primary resources—one a book, the other a library:

Tennessee History: A Bibliography, compiled and edited by Sam B. Smith and published in 1974 by the University of Tennessee Press, is without peer as a comprehensive sourcebook of written materials on the history of Tennessee.

The Tennessee State Library and Archives in Nashville is a rich treasury of materials on Tennessee history, containing census data, maps, county histories, genealogies, public records, books, periodicals, manuscripts, theses, and dissertations. The library has a complete photocopied and microfilmed duplicate of the entire remaining record of the Rugby colony—more than 5,000 items in all—and a complete microfilmed set of the Ruskin colony's newspaper, *The Coming Nation.*

Other libraries in the state with especially good resources on new communities in Tennessee history include the Metropolitan Nashville Public Library, the Memphis Public Library (the Memphis Room there has a good collection of materials on Nashoba), the University of Tennessee Library in Knoxville, and the Joint University Libraries in Nashville. The *Tennessee Historical Quarterly,* published by the Tennessee Historical Commission, is the most valuable periodical resource on the state's history. The files of daily newspapers in Tennessee's major cities are another good place to search for articles on the state's earliest communities.

A manuscript which parallels the theme of this book is *Some Tennessee Utopias,* by Ernest I. Miller. The bound typescript was issued by the Department of Sociology of the University of Tennessee in 1942 as a monograph.

For particular writings on the three communities featured in this book, the following are recommended:

NASHOBA

• William R. Waterman. *Frances Wright.* New York: Columbia University Press, 1924. The earliest biography of the founder of Nashoba.
• Alice J. Perkins and Theresa Wolfson. *Frances Wright, Free Enquirer.*

New York: Harper, 1939. Besides Waterman's, this is the only other comprehensive and scholarly biography of Wright.

• Richard Stiller. *Commune on the Frontier: The Story of Frances Wright.* New York: Thomas Y. Crowell, 1972. Presumably written for a young audience, this addition to Crowell's "Women of America" series has a good bibliography.

• Several of Frances Wright's published works and her collected lectures are available in some libraries, catalogued under her married name, D'Arusmont.

RUGBY

• Thomas Hughes. *Rugby, Tennessee.* New York: Macmillan, 1881. Included are letters Hughes wrote describing Rugby for readers of the *Spectator* in London and his address at the opening of the colony. A facsimile edition of the book was published in 1973 by the Rugbeian Press and Big Sink Books, and is available in many Tennessee bookstores and from the Rugby Restoration Association.

• Edward C. Mack and W. H. G. Armytage. *Thomas Hughes: The Life of the Author of "Tom Brown's School Days."* London: Benn, 1952. Probably the best biography of Hughes. Available at the Tennessee State Library, and at other libraries in the state.

• Booklets on the history of Rugby and its buildings by Brian L. Stagg *(The Distant Eden),* Sarah L. Walton *(Memories of Rugby Colony),* and Patricia Guion Wichman *(Christ Church, Episcopal, Rugby* and *Rugby: A Great Man's Dream)* are especially useful. All of them are in the state library collection and most of them can be purchased at Rugby.

RUSKIN

• Robert E. Corlew. *A History of Dickson County, Tennessee.* Nashville: Tennessee Historical Commission and Dickson County Historical Society, 1956. The rise and fall of Ruskin is well told in a 16-page chapter.

• Isaac Broome. *The Last Days of the Ruskin Co-operative Association.* Chicago: C. H. Kerr, 1902. An eyewitness account of the demise of Ruskin; available in the state library.

• The most recent detailed account of the Ruskin experiment was written in 1973 by Vera Gilmore. Copies of her unpublished thesis, "The Ruskin Colony, 1894–1901: Experimental Model for the Socialist Commonwealth," are in the state library and the University of Tennessee Library at Knoxville.

Index

The Tennessee communities, past and present, which are mentioned in this book are included in the index below. Those which still exist as place names and as active communities are designated by bold face type. Names of communities which no longer exist as names on the state map or as ongoing communities are enclosed in brackets.